Louise Wiggins

NO TIME FOR TOMBSTONES

Life and Death
in the
Vietnamese Jungle

No Time for Tombstones

LIFE AND DEATH IN THE VIETNAMESE JUNGLE

James and Marti Hefley

Christian Publications, Inc.
25 S. Tenth Street
Harrisburg, Penna. 17101

Library of Congress Catalog Card Number 74-80772.
ISBN 8423-4719-4 cloth; 8423-4720-8 paper.
Copyright © 1974 Tyndale House Publishers, Inc.,
Wheaton, Illinois. All rights reserved. First printing,
June 1974. Printed in the United States of America.

*To the
foreign missionaries
who remain
at their posts
in still-troubled
Viet Nam*

Explanation to Readers

In following a novelized form of writing non-fiction, the authors of this true story have taken dramatic license to supplement many incidents with imaginary conversation and details based upon their general research, and to use anonymous names for the various North Vietnamese officers and guards.

Contents

One Captured 1
Two Happy Valley 15
Three Fading Hope 27
Four Escape 39
Five Prisoners on Display 53
Six Sorrow on the Mountain 65
Seven Betty's Victory 75
Eight "Father, forgive . . . ." 85
Nine March of Death 95
Ten Moment of Destiny 105
Afterword 122
A Word of Thanks from the Authors 123

TET in the western year of 1968. Fireworks and feasts to celebrate the beginning of the Vietnamese "Year of the Monkey." A welcome truce proclaimed by the warring parties. A holiday from horror—hopefully.

CHAPTER 1

Captured

On *Tet* Eve, Monday, January 29, Vange Blood turned in bed and gently shook her husband awake. "Hank, that's awfully loud for firecrackers, don't you think?"

Hank lifted his head and listened. "I wouldn't worry. They get louder every year."

His reassurances to the contrary, the lanky Bible translator to the Mnong Rolom people was fully awake. There had been rumors that the Communists would try something big during *Tet*. He'd heard such stories in Kontum where he had taken their daughter Cindy to mission school. And the tribespeople in the Radê village where they lived on the southern outskirts of the highland town of Banmethuot had been warning the missionaries to leave.

He wondered if Vange had done the right thing in returning from Saigon so soon. She'd gone there to take their four-year-old Carolyn for an eye examination, taking along baby Cathy and leaving five-year-old David with him. She would have stayed longer if she had not felt sorry for them, left at home without a cook.

Boom!

"Mamma! Daddy!" Carolyn called.

"Go back to sleep, honey. It's *Tet*, remember."

Boom! Boom!

By 2:30 Tuesday morning the sounds of war were unmistakable—mortars pounding the South Vietnamese Army camp which was just up the hill. Machine guns rat-a-tat-tatting lethal messages. Stray bullets zinging overhead, too close for comfort.

"Let's get the kids into the bunker," Hank said in quick decision.

Grabbing the sleepy-eyed children, a flashlight, and some blankets, they rushed outside and scuttled into the dark hole. The small room below ground had a roof of logs and dirt that would ward off stray bullets and protect them from anything but a direct hit by a mortar.

They got the children settled and prayed. Then Hank began quoting his favorite Psalm for protection. *"The Lord is my light and my salvation; whom shall I fear? the Lord is the strength of my life; of whom shall I be afraid?"*

There was too much noise for anyone to sleep. They huddled together in the damp darkness, both trying to calm the growing fears of their children. "When daylight comes," Hank kept assuring them, "the VCs will go away. They always do."

Finally the mouth of the bunker began to whiten. They waited. They could see splashes of sun. But the bombardment continued as fierce as ever.

This was very serious.

Hank pulled his son toward him. He was so young, yet he wanted to be sure of David's relationship with the Lord. If the attackers should overrun the village, one grenade would be enough.

 The Bloods' nearest American neighbors were just two blocks above them. Christian and Missionary Alliance nurses Betty Olsen and Ruth Wilting lived in adjoining houses fronting Highway 14. Across the highway, which connected with Saigon 200 miles to the south, was the steepled Radê church and the main Christian and Missionary Alliance compound backing up to the military base. Here, trapped in their two-story Italian-style villas, were the Bob Ziemers, the Ed Thompsons, and father-daughter Leon and Carolyn Griswold.

Both Betty's and Ruth's roommates were away, so the girls had pooled their morale by staying together at Ruth's house during the night. Betty, 34 and the younger, had just dared a peep through the window. "Oh, dear God," she whispered in shock. "That wasn't a Vietnamese tank we heard explode during the night. It was the Griswolds' house!"

Seeing the destruction some hundred yards up the hill, her first impulse was to try and help any survivors. Then the self-possessed, trim redhead drew back. "They'd knock us down like pigeons, Ruth, if we try to go over there. The VCs are firing across the grounds at the ARVN base. There are probably more VCs in the church."

The girls retreated into Ruth's bedroom, where the shades were already drawn, to pray and wait for a lull in the shooting.

The minutes dragged by. After a while Betty broke the silence. "I've always told people I have no fear because I know I'm in the center of God's will. I'm not so sure I can say that now, though I know this is where God wants me."

Ruth nodded. "Yes, it's like when Dan, Archie, and Ardel were captured," she said referring to the abduction of her Mennonite fiancé and two Alliance co-workers in 1962. "After the VCs took them off, we spent a fearful night at the leprosarium before coming into town."

Betty glanced at Dan's boyish picture, framed on Ruth's dresser. "And we haven't heard from them since," she sighed.

Ruth's lip was trembling. "I know. But lately, I've had the strangest feeling that Dan and I are going to be reunited soon. I've been working on my wedding dress."

A bullet zinged by the wall, causing them both to duck involuntarily. The firing outside continued unabated for another hour or so. They kept straining to hear the whirr of helicopters. "They must have knocked the chopper base out of commission, or the boys would be here to help us," Betty finally concluded.

About ten the firing lessened, but still seemed too heavy to chance a run. Suddenly they heard a motor. Someone was coming in a vehicle.

Ruth took a quick look and pulled back in surprise. "Good grief, it's Mike Benge! That's his International Scout. There's a Vietnamese boy with him. Where are they going?"

"Some people don't have enough sense to be afraid. He must be planning on rescuing us," Betty replied with a wry grin.

The AID man was past the church now, moving cautiously toward the driveway to the compound.

"Look!" Ruth whispered excitedly. "Ed Thompson is waving from his window. He's trying to get Mike to turn back."

"There's his reason," Betty declared tensely. "A dozen VC are coming onto the road up ahead. Now Mike sees them and is backing up . . . Oh, no! More VCs are crawling out of the culvert behind Mike. They've got him. Oh, why did he have to pull such a stunt?"

There was nothing they could do but watch as Mike and

the boy were dragged from the Scout and marched down into the village, out of sight.

"He tried," Ruth said admiringly. "Mike may not be what some would like him to be. But he loves people and he's got courage."

"Yes," Betty agreed. "He's really a good guy. The best man AID ever had with the tribespeople. I wonder if we'll ever see him again."

Mike's capture lowered their spirits. The feisty, wise-cracking, crew-cut AID officer was hardly the answer to a maiden missionary's prayers, but he was liked and respected by all the missionaries. Among the American AID contingent in Viet Nam, he was known as a Montagnard "freak" because of his close identification with the jungle tribespeople, but he had been decorated twice for his achievements in education and agriculture.

By this time the Blood children were ravenously hungry and miserable in the cramped bunker. Their parents cautiously took them back into the kitchen. Hank pushed a table against the wall, piled a big foam mattress on top, and pushed the kids' single mattresses underneath. Here they could play with toys while Vange hastily assembled some food.

In late morning the gunfire slackened and the nurses saw Bob, Ed, and some tribal helpers pulling back wreckage from the Griswolds' house. "Carolyn and her father must still be in there," Betty said. "Let's chance it now."

Grabbing the small bags they'd already packed, the two slender single women sprinted across the highway and the debris-strewn lawn to where the men were working. "We heard Carolyn moaning," Bob Ziemer reported to them. "Leon is unconscious or dead. The rest of us are okay."

"Thank God for that," Betty murmured. "I'll go get a supply of medicine." Then she raced toward the clinic warehouse behind the church before anyone could stop her.

She returned safely. After more prizing and moving of timbers, the men were able to reach Carolyn, and they lifted her, still in her nightgown, from the wreckage. They carried her into the Ziemer house where the nurses determined that she had a broken right leg, internal injuries, and was in shock. But when they finally reached Leon Griswold, he was beyond help. They removed his body to the servants' house which stood between the Ziemers' villa and the fence enclosing the military base.

They talked about escape and discussed the possibility of getting Carolyn to a hospital. Y Ngue, the pastor of the Rade tribal church, had helped remove the Griswolds. He shook his head. "The VCs are still here. They're even in the church. I'll take my crippled son and try to get help in town. The VCs know us."

The pastor took his boy, Chen, and started toward the village, leaving two other sons, one 17 and one 10, with the missionaries. The oldest son's fiancée and her sister remained also.

Occasional firing punctuated the afternoon, then about six Hank Blood and his son David appeared. Hank was quickly informed of Leon Griswold's death and Carolyn's precarious condition, and that Pastor Ngue had gone for help but hadn't returned.

"Have you heard anything from MAC V [the American military advisers quartered near Banmethuot]?" Bob Ziemer asked.

Hank hadn't and speculated that both the American advisers and the helicopter pilots had been pinned down under the attackers' fire. He also surmised that the mission compound might be safer than his rented house in the Radê village below.

"I doubt it," Bob replied. "You're welcome to stay, but Pastor Ngue said the VCs were all around."

"Then we'd better get back. When dark comes, we'll probably get it."

Returning, Hank shepherded his family into the damp bunker. He and Vange had just made the children comfortable when their landlord's wife, with her eight children and three other relatives, wiggled in to join them. Throughout Tuesday night, they heard explosions all around. Some were close enough to shake the ground, showering the roof of the bunker.

After dark they heard planes and helicopters flying overhead. Apparently the Americans had fought off their attackers and were now in the action.

The situation remained just as critical at the Alliance compound. Betty and Ruth watched over Carolyn in one room, the Ziemers and Thompsons stayed in another, and the four Radê young people huddled in the servants' house where Leon Griswold's body had been stored.

When Wednesday morning came Carolyn was still unconscious and delirious. The nurses felt they should risk another dash to the clinic warehouse for more medicines and blood plasma.

The men protested that they should go. "No," Betty insisted. "You couldn't find anything. I've just inventoried our whole stock and can run in and out in a minute. Anyway, they're less apt to shoot women."

After Betty and Ruth returned safely, Bob and Ed painted a big SOS on an old door and placed it on top of a car. They hung out a white flag, then dug out the garbage pit behind the Ziemer house to have ready as a makeshift bunker. They were preparing to bury Leon Griswold in a shallow grave when war activity picked up.

From Bob and Marie's window they saw two black-pajamaed Vietnamese men wearing brown floppy hats shinny through a window into the Thompsons' house, then jump back out. A minute later the house blew apart in a tremendous explosion.

"This house will be next," Bob predicted. "We'd better join the Radês in the servants' quarters."

The others agreed and the men carried the still unconscious Carolyn on a cot into the small, one-story green house.

The Bloods had spent Wednesday in their house, mostly under the table, trying to keep the children reasonably content. When evening came, Hank and Vange decided to keep the children where they would be more comfortable. They feared they might cry in the crowded bunker and draw fire that would endanger the landlord's family.

About two A.M. Thursday Hank smelled bamboo burning. He looked through the shutters and saw that several neighboring houses were afire. Their house had concrete walls and a metal roof, so they were in no danger. But when the shutters on the storerooms in back caught fire, he ran out with a bucket of water and doused the flames.

"The VCs must not be too close," he said upon returning. "Nobody shot at me."

At last the children were asleep. Hank and Vange joined hands and waited. When dawn came, Vange served them breakfast under the table. At noon, they got their first news report on the radio: "The president of Viet Nam advises all people in Viet Cong-infiltrated areas to evacuate immediately."

"Let's make a break for it," Hank told Vange. "Pack some food while I check in back."

Seconds later Hank came panting back in and dived under

the table. "VC in the shower room! Shot at me. Heard the bullets whiz past my head. Now that they know Americans are here, they'll be in to get us. Nothing to do but pray."

His six-four frame bent under the table, the big ex-engineer from Portland began to pray as his wife had never heard him before.

"Lord God, you are all powerful. You control the courses of nations. Neither death nor life nor principalities nor powers can separate us from your love. You saved us and called us to give the Mnongs your Word. You brought Vange and me together. You gave us our children and healed them when they were sick. You brought us to Viet Nam and provided for our needs. You protected us at the lake when the enemy soldiers came. You kept watch over me when I hid in the pigpen just a few days ago. Nothing can harm us unless it is your will. Be our strong tower, our shield as the enemy draws near. Watch over our babies who are not old enough to understand. . . ."

Before he finished they heard voices and a hammering at the front door. "*Muc su* [preacher]," one called.

"Yes," Hank answered. "I am here."

A moment of silence passed. Perhaps they hadn't heard.

An explosion shook the house. Then came a second blast, throwing shrapnel into the kitchen. Vange cried out in pain as she took fragments in a leg and knee. Another piece creased the forehead of little Cathy, leaving her dazed.

Hank turned to Vange, quoting Proverbs 16:7: "When a man's ways please the Lord, he makes even his enemies to be at peace with him." Crawling out from under the table, he ran outside through the blown-out door, forcing a smile, hands in the air. Vange, carrying Cathy, followed by the other two children, came along behind him.

A black-pajamaed soldier motioned for them to get in a huddle on the ground. *This is it*, both Hank and Vange thought. But it wasn't. They checked Hank's pockets for a gun and asked if more Americans were in the house. One VC bandaged Cathy's head and Vange's leg. Two others tied Hank's arms behind his back with telephone wire.

"Americans, follow me," one of the Vietnamese commanded with a sweeping arm motion.

 The Alliance missionaries had fared worse. Somtime before dawn they had fled to the garbage pit, leaving Carolyn barely alive in the servants' house. When daylight came, Ruth and Betty decided to get more medicines and plasma for their patient. When they reached the clinic safely, Betty impulsively said, "I'm getting a car to take Carolyn to the hospital."

She ran to one of the mission vehicles and started the motor. Before she could shift into gear, a bullet smashed the windshield, narrowly missing her head. Communist soldiers surrounded the car. One opened the door. Another dragged her out and pulled her across the highway into the tribal section and across several back yards to the house where other captives were being held. She recognized Pastor Ngue, little Chen, and several lay leaders from the church.

A short while later Marie Ziemer staggered in, the left side of her dress soaked with blood. She slumped down beside Betty who began checking her wounds.

Marie looked dazed and weak, but was able to speak. "Bob ... with Jesus," she murmured. "Thompsons ... dead. Ruth, too, I think. They begged for mercy. The soldiers wouldn't listen ..."

Soon Hank and Vange were pushed inside with their frightened children clinging to them. They groped their way through the crowd to where Betty and Marie were huddled against a wall. Vange slipped down beside them, while Hank remained standing, holding their youngest child. Betty told them what had happened.

The little two-room house was so crowded the Americans could hardly move. The tribal captives and Hank Blood were bound with telephone wire. The translator towered above the others, his white face drawn.

They heard the whirr of a helicopter overhead, then its guns firing from a low altitude. One bullet slammed through the house and wounded a tribesman.

After the chopper left, an officer came in for Betty. He escorted her to the wrecked mission on the hill. She saw the bodies of the Thompsons and Ruth Wilting in the garbage pit. Bob Ziemer's body hung over a clothesline as he had fallen. As she was trying to move it to a cot, her escort asked, "Where is his gun?"

She exploded in bitter anger. "You fool, missionaries don't have guns!"

The Communist frowned. He refused to let her look at Carolyn or check on the bodies of the young Radês who were sprawled near the servants' quarters. "Get your bag, and come," he ordered. She grabbed the small package and hurried out.

The officer returned her to the crowded house where the Blood children were complaining of thirst. The guards brought a little water. Betty found more in a rice pan and strained it through a strip of Vange's slip. The youngsters drank it gladly.

As darkness approached, two soldiers came in with a bag of rice and several cans of food. The Bloods recognized the cans as having come from their house. But they were more concerned for Hank's language notes, representing eight years of study.

The officer pulled Hank aside. "Do you want to go back to America with your wife and children?"

"*Muon cho* [I sure do]!" Hank replied.

"Then give us your agency."

Hank didn't understand the question. He looked at Vange blankly, but she just shrugged her shoulders. She didn't understand either. The interrogator then took Hank outside.

They returned a few minutes later. "Go get your husband's papers," the officer ordered Vange.

Accompanied by the officer, Vange limped back to the house. The floors were strewn with books, papers, clothes, and toys, but she managed to find their passports and Vietnamese identity cards. She handed them to the officer.

They returned to the house, where all the prisoners were given a propaganda lecture on the "just cause of the National Liberation Front." A stern warning was given to make no noise; not even a match could be lit, nothing that might attract attention.

Vange was then ordered to make another trip to her home to get some extra clothing for Hank. She returned with a pair of trousers and two shirts.

"We're going to let your wife and children and the wounded missionary lady go," the officer told Hank. "You and the red-haired lady will come along with the Radê captives."

They began moving the captives out and Hank had only a few seconds to kiss his wife and children goodbye. "Kiss Cindy for me," he called to Vange as a soldier pulled him away. "And tell the gang the Lord has done a special work in my heart. I've surrendered everything to him."

They had tied Betty to Pastor Ngue with a loop of wire. Beside him stood his little son. "Come on! Come on!" the guards were yelling.

"Wait," the middle-aged tribal preacher begged. "Let the boy go."

"No," an officer declared. "He's young and can learn to follow the revolution."

The preacher reached and pulled up his son's trouser leg. "See how he has been burned by napalm. Have mercy," he begged. "Let him go back and study. Then you can teach him."

The officer pushed the boy away. "Very well, but if he talks, he is dead."

"Move!" the officer shouted, and the captives fell in line, Pastor Ngue and Betty walking together and behind them Hank Blood, his white face bobbing above the file of dark-skinned tribal captives.

CHAPTER 2

Happy Valley

After their capture, Mike Benge and the Vietnamese boy Ky had been taken to the Communist command post in the Radê village. There Mike was stripped of his wallet, watch, and prized brass bracelet, a gift from a Radê chief.

"*Chao ông Benge* [How are you, Mr. Benge]?" an officer asked.

"I'd be better if you'd let me take my friends to safety," Mike replied. "And how do you know my name?"

"Ah, we know all about you. You are an important official of the U.S. State Department. Sometimes you live in town with your American friends. Sometimes you go into villages to learn about the movements of the Liberation Army. In you, we have—how do you say it?—caught very big fish."

"Your informants are in error, sir. I am a civilian—a noncombatant helping the tribal people grow better crops. Ask any of them. They'll tell you."

"No, you are a spy for the imperialist American invaders."

Mike looked straight into the unsmiling face of his Vietnamese questioner. "You, sir, wear the uniform of the so-called National Liberation Front. But your accent tells me you are from North Viet Nam."

The face remained impassive. "I see you do not know Vietnamese very well. We are all from the south. North Viet Nam supports us politically, but has no soldiers in the south. Now if you will give us a little military information, perhaps we can be lenient with you."

Mike again emphasized that he was nonmilitary and added that he had no knowledge of battle plans or troop movements. Finally, after considerable interrogation, the North Vietnamese turned the American and his young companion over to guards.

Later that evening they joined a contingent of tribal captives for a forced march along a jungle road. When they arrived at a small military camp, Mike looked through the trees and recognized a familiar U-shaped building: the leprosarium operated by tribal nurses. The Alliance missionaries hadn't lived here since the capture of Dr. Ardel Vietti, Dan Gerber, and Archie Mitchell back in 1962. But Mike had made two or three risky jaunts into the jungle for visits and knew the place.

Nearby a crowd of fist-shaking Viet Cong were clustered around ten prisoners, hurling accusations in Radê. Mike had seen some of the prisoners around Banmethuot. Because he understood the Radê Montagnard dialect spoken by some 100,000 tribesmen in the Banmethuot area, he knew they were facing a Communist "people's court."

Powerless to intervene, Mike stood beside the thin Vietnamese boy and listened as the prisoners were sentenced to death. Then the hapless tribesmen were pushed before a firing squad. A volley of shots echoed through the jungle and ten bodies crumpled to the ground.

The shock was too much for Ky. The terrified boy broke into a run. As he dashed into some bushes, Mike heard the crack of a Russian-made AK-47 rifle, and a yelp of pain. A soldier walked out of the thicket and reported to the commanding officer, "He's hit in the leg. What shall we do with a wounded prisoner?"

"Kill him," the North Vietnamese officer snapped with cold casualness. The soldier ran back and fired again. The boy was quiet.

Mike felt as if he'd been kicked in the stomach. "Why did you have to do that?" he demanded recklessly. He was not easily frightened. He had broken wild horses and ridden rodeo bulls back in Oregon. He had taught policemen judo after serving in the U.S. Marines. Since coming to Viet Nam he had been marked for death because of his success in helping Montagnards. But now he felt the end had come. They had killed the boy. He would be next.

He waited in suspense before being taken aside for more grilling. Again he pointed out that the officers were North Vietnamese, despite their disguised clothing. Again this was denied.

He was held at the leprosarium until Thursday evening, then marched back toward Banmethuot. Early Friday morning, the column halted near the Radê cemetery which was just across a stream from the village where he had first been captured. He heard voices up ahead.

"Hey, Mike, are you okay?"

Hank Blood—speaking in Radê.

Mike gave a quick shake of the head and pursed his lips in a silent shhh. He didn't want their captors to know he understood Radê.

Behind Hank was perky Betty Olsen, tied with wire to Pastor Ngue. Farther back was a string of tribal prisoners, fifty or so.

Two helicopters fluttered overhead. Hank yelled and moved his body furiously before guards pulled him down. The choppers flew off, giving no indication the prisoners had been seen.

Herding the Americans together, the North Vietnamese hustled their prisoners back into the jungle.

When they stopped to regroup, one untied Pastor Ngue from Betty and handed him an unloaded machine gun to carry. When they moved on in single file Ngue stayed protectively close to Betty. About two kilometers from the cemetery, she saw him positioning the machine gun to strike the guard in front. "Oh, no, Pastor," she remonstrated. "We have to love our enemies and pray for them. You mustn't fight back!"

"*Vous êtes très naïve*," he muttered in reply, slipping into French, which was like a second mother tongue for him.

After four hours' hike they stopped near the leprosarium where Mike had witnessed the executions. The North Vietnamese seemed especially solicitous of the three Americans and gave them rice and monkey meat. The captives noticed that the tribal prisoners did not receive as much.

Pastor Ngue was still seething with anger, not over the food, but because the missionaries and church leaders had not been released. "We do not fight. We help people," he kept saying. "*Amai* [Sister] Betty is a nurse. I have seen her scraping the calluses from the feet of lepers. You will not win the allegiance of the people by taking her and us."

The commander was unmoved. "Why do you plead for the Americans? Don't you know they are enemies of the Vietnamese people?"

"Ha, you are the enemies who burn and kill and destroy."

"And you are the hands and feet of the American imperialists. The two men are CIA. The woman, we do not know who she is yet. If she is as you say, perhaps we will let her go. The National Liberation Front is just."

The officer withdrew to consult with his compatriots. The result was that the prisoners were divided into two groups, with Ngue being separated from the Americans and marched off ahead of them.

"Your friends will come searching for you," the North Vietnamese informed Betty, Hank, and Mike. "We are moving you to another area for questioning."

He looked at Betty's street shoes, scuffed and battered from the 12-mile walk to the leprosarium. Her legs were splattered with red mud and her thin print dress was tattered and torn. "We will show pity to you. Put on these combat boots. They were taken from an enemy whom we executed yesterday."

The painful wire was removed and she rubbed her wrists to restore circulation. Then she changed to the heavy, cumbersome boots and got in line behind Mike, whose hands had been freed also.

The North Vietnamese pushed them rapidly along the narrow trail, making communication difficult. During a brief rest stop Betty and Hank managed to tell Mike about the massacre.

"Vange and the baby were slightly injured," Betty said. "They'll be okay. I doubt if Marie Ziemer will make it. I think Carolyn will live if she gets proper medical care. What about your people, Mike?"

"The infiltrators shot up the town Monday night. I think everybody got out the next morning. I dropped an AID nurse off at the province hospital, then came looking for you guys."

"And got yourself captured," Hank added dryly.

"All in the line of duty. Say, do you know what happened to Pastor Ngue's boys?" Mike queried. "He was asking me back at the leprosarium before they separated us."

"The crippled one they let go as we were leaving," Hank recalled.

Betty hesitated, then said, "When I went back to the compound to get my things, I saw bodies lying all over. I'm pretty sure two of them near the servants' quarters were his boys. The guard wouldn't let me examine them."

"Did you tell the preacher?" Hank asked.

"No. I thought of it once when we were tied together. But I'm not positive, so there was no need to upset him. Besides he might get so angry that he'd kill someone."

The column moved again. They walked at a rapid pace until an hour or two after nightfall when they were allowed to wash in a stream. Then Betty was given her bag.

"Mike, Hank!" she called. "They took the clinic money! When I went back to the compound I stuffed it in here—at least $3,000."

Mike called the officer and explained what had happened. He admitted the bag had been opened and searched, but denied vehemently that any money had been taken.

"Well, at least they didn't take my Bible," Betty said, though she was still upset over the mission funds.

Bowls of white rice were brought, and after eating, the captives were chained together at the ankles and made to lie on mats near several guards. There was only enough time for Hank to quote some Bible verses and to pray before a stern voice ordered quiet. Despite the strain of the past days, they fell into exhausted sleep.

The chains were removed the next morning. After breakfast the soldiers hurriedly broke camp and got everyone moving again. There seemed to be fewer tribal captives than the night before. Mike was sure some had escaped during the night.

At midmorning they started across a precarious log bridge over a steep ravine. Hank kept his eyes straight ahead and crossed with no difficulty. The steely-nerved Benge looked to see how deep it was. Impressive, but he'd seen more treacherous crevices. He hurried to keep up with long-legged Hank.

Then he heard a pitiful wail, and a sickening thud. *Betty!* he thought, whirling around and running back down the trail. Looking into the gorge he saw that her fall had been broken by another log about ten or twelve feet down.

"Are you all right?" he called.

"I—I think so," Betty replied weakly. "I lost my glasses; they fell clear to the bottom."

"Never mind that. If you don't have any broken bones it

will be a miracle. Hold on, we'll get a rope."

The hovering guards gave Mike a rope. He tied it around his middle and scrambled down the side of the ravine to help her. Cautiously she got up, holding on to Mike for support.

"Sure you're all right?" he asked solicitously.

"Yeah, I just got the breath knocked out of me."

With help from some of the other prisoners, who pulled on the rope, they made it up the bank. A couple of tribesmen scrambled down the steep incline to look for her glasses. A gleeful shout announced success.

"Praise the Lord," Betty said. "I really appreciate your effort in searching for them," she told the delighted Radê who returned them to her.

"*Mau di!*" commanded one of the guards, "Move fast!"

"Can't you give her a minute to catch her breath?" Mike asked indignantly.

"We've wasted enough time already. Move on!"

Later that afternoon they stopped at a small military encampment. The Americans were given toothpaste, brushes, soap, and mercurochrome for scratches and were permitted to clean up. The tribal captives were ordered into the woods to cut poles. Under the supervision of the North Vietnamese, two small pole cages were hastily constructed and placed about forty feet apart. Hank and Betty were put in one and Mike in the other. Then their chains were secured and padlocked for the night.

Hank and Betty agreed that they should be as open as possible with their captors. "We have nothing to hide," the Bible translator said. "Surely they'll release us when they know why we're in Viet Nam."

The camp commander, who introduced himself as Captain Son, took Hank out the next day for interrogation.

"Tell us what your employer does," he began.

Hank tried to explain how the Wycliffe Bible Translators worked. "We are linguists, translating the Bible into tribal languages. We serve in Mexico, Peru, Ecuador, New Guinea, the Philippines, Viet Nam, and several other countries. We would work in North Viet Nam if your government would permit us. My wife and I are with the Mnong Rolom group that live near Banmethuot. For a while we lived in a village, but your 'friends' made this too dangerous. We had to move into the Radê village close to town."

"That is the only reason you are in Viet Nam?" Captain Son said in evident disbelief.

"Yes, sir. When we finish the translation and it is published, we will leave. Oh, perhaps we may do some literacy work and train some teachers. But this will only be so the Mnongs can read about God and his Son, Jesus."

"How are you supported? Who pays your salary?"

"We don't have a salary. As God leads, Christian friends and churches in the United States send money to our main office. This comes to us. It's just enough to pay our necessities. If you will ask the soldiers, who searched our house, they'll tell you we live very simply. We're not here for profit but to serve God and help the Mnong people have God's Word in their own language."

"An incredible story. But go on. How do you feel about us —the National Liberation Front, and our program of revolution?"

"We don't involve ourselves with anyone's politics. We will help you, as we will help any other Vietnamese individual. If you oppose us, we cannot fight back. God tells us to love even our enemies."

"God? Ha, Ha! You are stupid to say there is a God. Where is he? Why does he not set you free? There is no God. Revolution is power. Man forms his own destiny. We are the supreme being."

"You have been misled, Captain. God has power over all of us."

"Then why doesn't he help you?"

"He will. His Book says that man's ways are not his ways, nor man's thoughts his thoughts. He doesn't forget his people. He has allowed you to take us for some purpose. Perhaps that you may hear of him. We are his witnesses."

"You are CIA. Or crazy. Maybe both. I will talk to the woman now."

Captain Son had the mild-mannered Hank put back into the cage and Betty brought out.

"When will you let us go?" she demanded in a no-nonsense tone.

"That will be our decision," he replied coldly.

"Don't you know I'm a nurse? There are wounded and sick civilians who need my care. Now that my friends are dead, the leprosy patients depend on me. If your movement is as you claim, you will let us go so we can help the people."

"I said we will decide when you can go. You will answer my questions. Give me your agency and how you are paid."

Betty traced the history of the Christian and Missionary Alliance in Southeast Asia, pointing out that the group had once had missionaries in North Viet Nam. "I am paid much less than I would receive as a nurse in the United States," she added. "We missionaries are not here for money or political intrigue. We're here to serve God and help people.

"Do you know of Dr. Vietti, the lady doctor who was captured by your people at the jungle hospital six years ago? She was taken with two men missionaries."

The North Vietnamese officer denied any knowledge of the abduction. "I have never heard this name," he insisted.

"After she and the two others were taken, we had to move to Banmethuot. Your friends wouldn't permit us to live close to the people. But we continued to send medicines out by tribal people. I'm sure we've treated some of your supporters."

Captain Son was unmoved. "How can I understand this? It is strange that a healthy lady should be out here alone, so far from home. Where is your husband?"

Betty fought to remain calm. "I don't need a husband to serve God."

Irritated, the officer ordered Betty back into her cage, then turned his attention to Mike.

The AID man was just as insistent that they be released. "I

am not military," he declared. "For five years I've been helping the tribespeople improve their economy. You have people in this camp who know me. Ask them."

"We know about you. You are here to spy on the people and the patriotic activities of our National Liberation Front."

"You are not in the N.L.F.," Mike again pointed out. "You are from North Viet Nam. Admit it."

The officer stared off into the jungle for a few seconds. Then he turned back and stared intensely at Mike. "So. Maybe we are from the north. Maybe we have come to help our brothers unify Viet Nam. That is not why you are here."

The North Vietnamese now turned the questioning back on Mike, demanding that the AID man give military information, and repeating the charge that he was CIA. Mike stood his ground, trading charge for charge, demanding that the stolen mission money be returned. The officer dismissed him in disgust.

After two weeks at this encampment, they were moved a few miles to another camp. Here all three Americans were put in a pole cage together, giving them the first opportunity to talk freely and at length.

"I was going to ask him for my Radê brass bracelet they took off my wrist," Mike said angrily. "It was given to me by the headman at Buon Kram when I was adopted into the tribe. I wouldn't have traded it for anything."

"Ask him the next time he comes over," Betty suggested. "He'll probably deny that it was taken."

"And that our watches were stolen too," Mike added, still seething inside.

Mike then speculated that they'd been moved to evade a search party. "I'm sure some Radês got away. They would have people out looking for us."

"If they don't find us, do you think we'll be allowed to go?" Betty asked.

Mike shrugged. "Who knows the minds of these people? They haven't been too hard on us. They've been feeding us."

"Yes. One fellow has been quite neighborly to me," Hank

said optimistically.

"Does either of you have any idea where we are?" Betty asked.

"We're about forty miles south of Banmethuot," Mike replied. "This area is Chu Rulach. Some call it Happy Valley, though I don't know why. It's been a Viet Cong stronghold for a long time."

"Could we escape?"

"Not the way they keep us padlocked in these chains. We'll just have to hope they'll see that it's to their advantage to let us go."

"We've been praying, Mike," Hank said. "I hope you'll join us."

Mike looked uncomfortable. "I've been a little out of touch since I was a boy."

"Tell us about it," Betty urged.

"Not much to tell. I grew up on a ranch in eastern Oregon. Near the little town of Heppner. You're from Portland, aren't you, Hank?"

Hank nodded.

"Well, uh, I went to a Lutheran church. Had four years of parochial school. Then like a lot of boys, I guess I sort of dropped out. Didn't go to church much in high school. Then came college at Oregon State, and—"

"You went to State?" Hank interrupted. "I got my degree in engineering there. So did my brother Dave."

"Small world. I finished a little later after a stretch in the Marines. Spent most of that time in Japan. Then I thought I'd try for the foreign service. Had to settle for International Voluntary Services at $77 a month. That was the forerunner of the Peace Corps. When my term was up for IVS, I got on with AID. That was in '65, three years ago last month. January 31st to be exact, the day after they grabbed me on the highway."

"Speaking of grabbing, here comes Captain Son and some strangers."

The North Vietnamese officer was smiling. "Good evening.

I hope you are feeling well. These visitors are artists and would like to sketch your pictures."

"Why?" Betty asked.

"To show others how well you are being treated."

"May we have some to take back with us?"

"Perhaps, Miss Olsen."

"And could I have one of your flags and a pair of Ho Chi Minh sandals for souvenirs?"

The officer was still smiling. "We might arrange that. If you pledge to be good."

"Oh, we'll all be good," Betty smiled hopefully. Her companions nodded in agreement. Maybe they would be released soon.

CHAPTER 3

Fading Hope

They had been with the North Vietnamese three weeks now and every morning they hoped that day would be the last. The starvation diet of rice, manioc, and occasional vegetables had made all three ravenously hungry. Though there were no roads in the wild, forested area, Mike was sure he could lead the way back to Banmethuot.

"I'm ready to go," Hank said. "After eight years, Vange and I were just getting ready to start translating books of the Bible. We had three language informants lined up to help, and now this," he sighed. Then he added quickly, "I'm sure the Lord has a purpose in our being here."

Mike and Betty were silent, content to listen to their talkative companion. Day after boring day there hadn't been much else to do in the debilitating heat except talk and listen. Captain Son had even denied them the privilege of writing letters.

"Our biggest frustration was not being able to live in a Mnong village," Hank went on. "We started out in Lac Thien, not too far from here. You've been there, I guess, Mike."

"Yeah, I know the place. Hasn't been secure for years."

"We were there back in 1960 when the Viet Cong were still called the Viet Minh. Just a short time . . . until one night the Minh came charging in, shooting up the village, looking for the district chief. Vange and I picked up Cindy and hid in a storeroom. We could hear them knocking around and talking in the other side of the house. We stayed there until 2:30 the next afternoon, just to be certain they'd left. I was pretty mad. They had killed three people, burned seven buildings, and stolen everything they could get their hands on. We had prayed hard for our friend the chief, and the Lord answered double. The chief dropped through a trap door and made it to the lake, where he escaped in a dugout. On the other side of the lake he walked into a little store where he thought he had friends. Turned out they were enemies. Two Minh tried to shoot him, but their guns failed to go off. Had to be the Lord.

"After that, the provincial authorities said we couldn't live there any more. We had to move into the Radê village close to Banmethuot and depend on language informants coming to us."

"Didn't you go back out just before Christmas?" Betty asked.

"Yeah, but not for long," Hank smiled grimly. "This was another Mnong village. One that had never been attacked. I wanted to do some checking on Luke 15 so we could prepare a small booklet. The first evening I went with the chief to a friend's house where a dozen or so Mnongs were sitting around drinking their rice wine."

"Mmmmmm. Good stuff," Mike interrupted with a chuckle, drawing a small frown from Betty.

"I guess it keeps you awake," continued Hank, "for at ten o'clock they were still gabbing and I was about to fall asleep. The chief had just taken me home when the shooting broke loose. I knocked out the kerosene light and ran around looking for a place to hide. I ended up in the chief's pigpen, pressed between two bundles of grass. The VCs overran the village, but they never found me. They did get my cameras and my favorite picture of Vange.

"When I got home, I tried to figure out what the Lord wanted to accomplish in that experience. I decided he wanted me to feel more sympathy for people who live out in villages and are exposed to attack night after night. And to impress on me the uncertainty of life so that I'd be more concerned about the spiritual condition of people I meet."

Hank paused and shifted his hip, careful not to hurt his companions by pulling too hard on the chains.

Then he looked directly at his fellow Oregonian. "Mike, are you sure of going to heaven when you die?"

"I'm not counting on dying soon," the AID man drawled laconically.

"Tough as you are, you may outlive both of us. But nobody can be sure."

"I respect you missionaries," Mike said. "You want to help the Radês and Mnongs and other tribespeople. So do I. I may be going at it in slightly different ways from you."

"And we respect you too, Mike," Betty broke in. "You're one of the best friends the people ever had, and us, too. I've heard Bob Ziemer and Ed Thompson say many times that if they needed something—cement, plane reservations, or whatever—you're the one to be counted on."

"Wycliffe people feel the same way," Hank said. "But what I'm asking, Mike, is: Do you really know the Lord? Are you sure he's forgiven your sins? If not, you won't go to heaven."

"Well, I don't think one person can judge another. I drink

a little. When I'm with the natives, I take my turn at the wine-jar. Makes them feel I'm one of them."

"I don't think that's necessary to gain their friendship," Betty interrupted.

"Jesus drank, didn't he? I've never been much of a Bible student, so correct me if I'm wrong in saying that the Bible teaches moderation."

"Yes, but Bible times were different from today," Hank interjected. "The wine was weak and there wasn't much water."

Mike suddenly burst out laughing. "Excuse me, but I was thinking of the first time I saw you, Betty. Remember that party at the AID nurses' house. I had been out in the village and came in half snockered. I was dancing with the AID gals and having a real good time. You missionaries were sitting there looking like you'd swallowed a jar of sour pickles."

"And you stopped and came over and asked if we wanted some drinks. Yes, I remember. We really thought you were far out. Now that I've gotten to know you better, I don't think you're that bad."

"Then you'll join me for a little celebration, when we get back?" Mike teased.

"Maybe we'll learn something about that now," Betty said hopefully. "Here comes Captain Son."

"How are you faring? Are you well?" the officer asked in mock politeness.

"We'd be better if you'd unlock these chains and send us away," Mike said.

"Perhaps tomorrow, Mr. Benge. Since you are civilians, I don't think we'll keep you much longer."

The captives' eyes lit up. This was the most reassuring word they'd had yet.

"Where are you keeping Pastor Ngue?" Betty asked.

"He is in another camp."

"Will he be given his freedom? And the other tribesmen?"

"I cannot say. All depends." The officer turned away, leaving the Americans to wonder and wait.

The day ended with a trip to the stream to wash up, and the evening meal. Betty marked the date—Saturday, March 2—on the tiny calendar she was keeping. She also managed to add a little to her diary.

The next day they held worship services. Hank gave an exhortation for patience, stressing that God didn't operate by man's schedules, assuring them that in good time his purposes for their experiences would be shown. Then Betty described how God had allowed Daniel to be thrown into a den of lions, and then had delivered him. Hank began his favorite hymn, "Lead On, O King Eternal," and concluded with a long, impassioned prayer. His plea that his wife and children be kept from harm brought tears to Betty and Mike.

Early Monday they were awakened by unmistakable artillery fire. Immediately they heard Captain Son barking shrill commands at his soldiers to break camp and march. Two men ran over and opened the door of their cage and unlocked their chains. Betty had just enough time to grab her bag and Bible, and Hank the small shaving kit he'd been allowed to keep.

They were pushed at a rapid pace all day. That night they camped under a thick grove of trees, and then were forced to move on before daybreak.

They kept up this pace for the next ten days, sometimes marching at night and sleeping during the day. Several times they heard planes overhead, but the thick forest cover blocked any view. From the sun, they judged they were moving west into the mountains that tower 8,000 feet, between Banmethuot and the coastal city of Nhatrang.

In Happy Valley they had benefited from vegetables bought by the North Vietnamese from farmers a day's journey away. But on the trail captors and captives alike had to supplement meager rice rations with occasional catches of frogs, lizards, monkeys, and mouse deer. Some days the Americans got no protein at all.

Near the end of the grueling trek they stopped in a small

tribal settlement. The soldiers bought pumpkins, corn, and beans from tribesmen in loin cloths and enjoyed a feast while the Americans stood by with stomachs growling.

Then, ignoring the soldiers, the headman of the village walked over to the white strangers. "How are you?" he asked kindly.

"Hungry," Mike replied in Radê. "Weak."

Without asking permission of the North Vietnamese commander, the tribesman immediately began gathering food for the captives. They enjoyed their first satisfying meal since leaving Happy Valley.

At the end of the next day's journey, the North Vietnamese set up camp in the fog on the side of a mountain. The altitude was higher here and the air colder. Nights were especially damp.

They were still kept chained at night, but the guards were more talkative. Some were Viet Cong whom the North Vietnamese had picked up along the trail.

One VC ventured to ask Mike how many letters they had written to their families. When Mike said this hadn't been permitted, he seemed surprised.

"There's a communications gap here," Mike told Betty and Hank. "The NVAs must have told these fellows we'd been allowed to write home."

The effects of improper nourishment began plaguing Hank first. Scales formed on his lower back and began spreading downward. An ugly boil swelled on his hip that made sleep difficult. He asked Betty to lance it with the razor, but she objected. "It isn't ready."

Sharp, sudden pains near his vertebral column in the small of the back were the worst. When these occurred at night, he would cry out in anguish, bellowing like a wounded buffalo and awakening his companions and their guards. Mike and Betty were sympathetic, but after the second attack the guards became angry and threatened punishment. Hank thought it was a recurrence of kidney stones, a problem he'd had three years before.

Mike, Betty, and Hank all had bruised feet. Betty's legs were covered with small ulcerous sores. Her skin and Mike's became scaly from lack of proper food. In addition, they all were plagued by the highly contagious parasitic skin disease caused by the itch mite. They itched all over. "If I ever get out of here," Betty moaned, "I'll never again take a hot bath for granted."

All three came down with dengue fever about the same time. Having passed through mosquito-infested lowlands a week before, they weren't surprised. Their bodies ached as if their bones were crumbling into little pieces. Their temperature roller-coastered up and down between high fever and chills. After three or four days they felt better, but a day later their temperatures rose again and they broke out in body rash. "The only good thing about dengue," Betty said, "is that it's almost never fatal. If for us you can call that good."

Except for the mercurochrome and a couple of sulfa pills Betty had been given to rub in her leg ulcers, they'd had no medicine. They knew there were remedies in the camp, for they'd seen soldiers treating one another. But their pleas for aid went unheeded. The best they could do was wash in the stream.

One evening after they had cleaned up, they lay under the soft half moon waiting for their chains to be padlocked. Betty recalled the return of a Vietnamese medical worker who had been abducted with a group of Radês at the leprosarium.

"He said they had to wear the same clothes they were captured in and never took them off. They weren't allowed to bathe and became covered with body lice which gave them sores all over their bodies. He still had the scars when I saw him two months after release. They had to work when they were sick, even when they had malaria. The only water they had to drink came from buffalo wallows. He said many died, especially children, and that if it hadn't been for the Lord, he would have given up. When I saw him and heard his story, I thought, 'How horrible,' never thinking that one day I'd be in practically the same fix."

"Yeah, well, they haven't made us do any work, and malaria hasn't got us—yet," Mike grimaced.

"Unless our 'protectors' have a change of heart soon, we may get malaria," Betty predicted. "Scurvy, beriberi and who knows what else?"

"Back in Happy Valley, Captain Son was talking about letting us go. Then the war got too hot for them," Hank said. "What do you think will happen now?"

"I don't know, but they've got no reason to hold us. I've told them that over and over. Now they've stopped hinting."

"Yeah, Betty," Mike said, "you've talked tougher to them than either Hank or I. As a woman you can get away with it."

Captain Son and a guard approached. "Time to sleep," the officer said indifferently.

Betty stood up and fastened her green eyes on the NVA. "Captain, have you ever dug pus and maggots out of the sores of lepers? Have you scraped the calluses off of infected feet until your finger joints ached and your knees became raw from kneeling on the floor? Have you peeled back the burned skin of babies who were the innocent victims of war?"

The North Vietnamese stood speechless, unable to reply.

"I have. All day and often into the night. Six days at a stretch, resting only on Sunday and then sometimes having to care for emergency cases. That's why I came to Viet Nam. Not for pleasure or to spy. But to heal the sick in the name of Jesus. And you, who make speeches about justice for the poor and giving land to the landless—what have you done? Taken me and my friends prisoner. Given us no medicine. Kept us chained like animals at night. Marched us through the forest until our feet were ready to fall off. If you had any compassion for the suffering people of Viet Nam, you would make us well and set us free to do our work."

Breathing hard, her face red with the ugly rash, she paused to let him reply. But Captain Son seemed interested only in watching the guard fasten and secure the chains around Hank and Mike's ankles. "Please sit down," he then asked Betty.

"Not yet," she said firmly. "I have more to say. I don't know why you continue to keep us. It must be orders from higher up. Whatever the reason and whatever you do, we will not hate you. We will feel pity. We will help you when we can. The God you say does not exist loves you. And we love you."

"Please sit," he again commanded.

"Yes," she said meekly. "I hope you will think of what I said."

The North Vietnamese didn't reply. He merely waited until the guard had fastened Betty's chains, then walked stolidly away.

A few mornings later they awoke to find Captain Son and his North Vietnamese underlings gone. Their guards were now all Viet Cong. A short distance away they saw other newcomers under the trees. Then they heard a familiar voice.

"It's Pastor Ngue," Betty said in joyful surprise. "I'd know him anywhere. I've heard him preach so many times. Pastor Ngue, over here," she called.

Ngue started in their direction and was rudely pulled back by a Viet Cong who shouted, "Go and dig manioc with the rest."

Later in the day, Ngue was permitted to talk with his American friends. He was appalled that they hadn't been given medicine and was especially troubled at Betty's sores. "I will try to find medicine in the forest," he promised.

The next morning when he went on the work detail to dig manioc roots, the Radê preacher slashed a few strips of bark from a cinnamon tree. After boiling the bark in water, he poured the solution into a bamboo cup and left it beside a rock for Betty. The soothing medicine applied to their sores was a great relief to all three Americans.

Unfortunately, Ngue was seen the next time he dropped the cup near Betty.

"What did you give her?" the Viet Cong head of the guards demanded.

"Medicine for their sores. You wouldn't do anything."

"Why are you helping these enemies of the Vietnamese people?"

"They haven't taken our land," Ngue remonstrated. "It is the North Vietnamese who have invaded."

"The Americans have deceived you. They and their Saigon puppets want to take all the land. The missionaries are their agents."

"No, the missionaries have no politics. They work only for God." The tribal preacher's nostrils were flaring, his eyes flashing.

"Bah! There is no God but Ho Chi Minh. He's our god—our leader."

Ngue pointed a finger. "Be careful about that. The Germans made Hitler a god. Now he's dead and disgraced."

"You, Ngue, are a fool. Quit following the Americans and support the revolution."

"I will follow no one but God and what I read in his Book. You are the fool."

The officer looked around and saw the guards were listening with intense interest.

"Stop your mouth," he commanded. "When the revolution is victorious, we will exterminate you preachers first. We would kill you now, except you are needed for work. Stop meddling and keep away from the American spies."

But Ngue was a stubborn and determined tribesman. He felt a fatherly responsibility toward Betty, whose own father was serving as a missionary in Africa. When he heard her crying at night, it was almost more than he could bear.

Risking possible execution, he slipped over to the little bamboo house where she lay chained with Mike and Hank.

"*Amai* Betty, don't cry," he whispered consolingly. "God will take care of us. I will pray."

Softly he began to talk to God in his native language, calling the names of Betty and the two American men, Hank's wife and children, remembering his own family, including the two who he did not yet know were dead. He also prayed for the Banmethuot congregation, that it would experience revival, that leaders would be found to direct the people in his absence. And for Ardel Vietti, Dan Gerber, and Archie Mitchell, the 1962 captives.

When he finished, there was no sound but the snoring of the guards a dozen paces away. Then a pathetic, little-girl voice broke out of the darkness. "Pastor Ngue, please help us get away."

"Shhhhh," he cautioned his "daughter." He sat and thought a long while, then leaned back to speak through the bamboo wall. "Tomorrow night. I will alert our tribal friends. We will hide sticks of wood. When the guards are sleeping we will pound their heads." His voice trailed off in bitter anger.

"No, no, no, Pastor. You cannot hurt them. They don't know the Lord. There must be another way."

Sadly he replied, "No, *Amai* Betty, there is no other way. But if you do not wish it, we will not try."

CHAPTER 4

Escape

About ten days after entrusting the Americans to Viet Cong guards, Captain Son and his North Vietnamese cadre returned to camp for a few hours.

"Are you being treated well?" he asked them.

Mike eyed him stonily. Hank looked away sadly. Neither replied.

"No, we have always been treated badly," Betty said. "It is wrong to keep people in chains who have done nothing but help your Vietnamese brothers. When can we go?"

"Are you receiving enough to eat?"

"Harrumph!" Mike snorted sarcastically.

"I have work to do," Betty continued. "Sick people are depending on me to come back. Would you rather I stay here and they suffer?"

"Very well, then," the Captain said turning on his heel to leave. "Since you need nothing from me..."

"Captain, we need meat," Hank pleaded. "And Miss Olsen must have a change of clothing. Most of all we need medicine."

Face had been saved for the officer. "I will ask my brothers to increase your rations. But we have no clothes for the lady. The medicine is reserved for our fighting men."

He walked away.

The food was better for a few days. They had boiled crabs once for lunch and monkey meat two evenings. And they received larger portions of rice. They were even unchained for part of each day and permitted to walk around the camp under the watchful eyes of the guards.

Mike wandered over to the cookhouse where several tribal prisoners were peeling manioc and pounding rice. In conversation he discovered their rations were pitifully small. "We will share with you," he promised.

The Americans began saving portions from each meal, which Mike took and hid in the cookhouse for their tribal friends.

The tribesmen did not forget. Two or three days later they returned from foraging in the forest with a bundle of plants. "For you," they told Mike. Mike took the plants gratefully for they had been denied greens lately.

By this time the dengue fever had subsided, but their bodies still burned from the fiery itch. Hank's boil was bigger and redder. Betty now feared that lancing might bring on infection. And the excruciating pains that struck Hank without warning continued to double him up.

They kept up their morale by reading from Betty's Bible, now soggy from being rained on. Hank memorized from a handful of soiled Scripture cards he had managed to keep. They prayed together two and three times a day with Mike joining in awkwardly. The two missionaries now sensed a change in the wiry AID man. He was quieter and not as cocky and flippant as he had been back in Happy Valley.

Hardly a day passed without the zealous Hank sharing with Mike about a personal relationship to God. To Mike's question, "How can I be sure?" Hank told how he had made certain himself at the age of fifteen.

"My family was in church every time the doors opened. My parents were Sunday school teachers. My mother even taught Greek at a Bible college. My brother Dave and I made professions of faith and were baptized as young boys. But when I was fifteen I became very worried about life after death. Would I go to heaven or to hell? Was I God's child or not? I wasn't sure. As I thought about what to do, I remembered John 1:12: 'As many as received him to them gave he power to become the sons of God.' I knew this was speaking of receiving Christ, so that night I told God, the best I knew how, that I was receiving Christ and his salvation. I said, 'God, I know you don't lie. I am taking you at your Word.' "

After pausing to let this sink in, Hank added forcefully, "I've never had any real doubts since."

"That's the only way," Betty put in quietly. "You can't save yourself by all the good you do for people. You have to look to the Savior who died on the cross for our sins."

Mike said nothing, but stared into the thick foliage, deep in thought, as old memories of his childhood flashed through his mind. How long had it been—was it really twenty-five years ago that he'd sat in the little Lutheran church in eastern Oregon and heard about Jesus? He remembered being hit by a car when in the first grade. He could have been killed then. And his mother had told him he was sickly before that. Why had he lived when other children had died?

He had determined to be tough. Playing high school football with boys taller and heavier. Pulling more than his weight among rugged loggers. Riding anything that had four legs and hair on its back. Joining the Marines. Mastering the art of judo so he could easily handle a man twice his size. Then after the Marines and college, coming to help the tribespeople in Viet Nam's Central Highlands.

Most American military counted the days until their year

was in 'Nam, but this civilian had stayed on, even after hearing that the VC had a price on his head. Once they had almost gotten him in an ambush. He had turned the corner as they were setting up, and gotten the draw on them first. If he'd been five minutes later... Why hadn't he? Why had he survived when friends, both military and civilian, had been shot down in the jungle?

Now, after two months in jungle captivity, he was still alive. He had thought his number was up when they had so ruthlessly killed the Vietnamese boy back by the leprosarium. But they had let him live. Why?

And in this situation, how much longer could he and his friends survive? Hank, Betty, and the Radê preacher were surely in touch with God. But was he? What was that verse Hank had quoted? "To as many as received Jesus." Certainly he could rely on that. Maybe he had believed in Sunday school. Maybe not. What counted was that he wanted to believe and rest in God's love and care *now*.

When he confided this to Hank and Betty, they rejoiced over his commitment.

Blustery March blew into cloudy April. Betty marked each day on her calendar. On April fifth Hank recalled that he and Vange had sailed out under the Golden Gate Bridge just ten years before. "We were in such a hurry that we didn't get hitched until we reached the Philippines," he said.

"Isn't Vange from Pennsylvania? And you're from Oregon. Where did you two get together?" Betty asked.

Hank grinned. "In Wycliffe's jungle training camp in Mexico where my brother Dave and I were outnumbered by the single girls. One of the fellows, Paul Marsteller, passed word along that Vange thought a lot of me. My first reaction was that this wasn't the way the Lord worked. Then I decided that he might have to use this means for somebody as bashful as me. I was already thirty-eight.

"The people supervising our training conveniently assigned Vange and me to the same raft crew. Four of us built and launched it for the test trip down river. Turned out it was too small, so the other two let Vange and me go alone. A hundred feet from the bank we started to sink. We paddled back and unloaded some cargo and started again. When we arrived a half hour behind the other rafts, they 'punished' us by making us set the pace on a 25-mile survival hike. Vange did fine, but I came down with an infected ankle and had to ride a mule with Dave leading it and Vange walking behind."

"You figured Vange could make it in Viet Nam, huh?"

"I sure did, Mike. But neither Dave nor I has ever been one to make quick decisions. I prayed about her every day and after we left camp in the spring we wrote regularly. On July 3rd—I remember the place—I prayed the prayer of faith and claimed her for my own. A little later she accepted my proposal and the following April she sailed with Dave and me. Dave and I had always done things together."

"Was Dave married then?" Betty asked.

"No. He had his eye on a single girl in our party. But they didn't really get together until after arriving in Viet Nam. He and Doris were married in Saigon. They're working with the Chams. As you know, the Chams are modern-day representatives of an ancient Indianized kingdom in Central Vietnam. And knowing Dave, I'm sure he's doing all he can to get us released."

"If you were married in the Philippines," Betty ventured, "where did you spend your honeymoon?"

"Probably on a jungle trail," Mike interjected.

Hank laughed. "Not quite. We shared a little summer cottage with some rats. Had a beautiful view, though, out there in the mountains among the Ifugao tribespeople. While there we did a little carpenter work for a couple of single girl translators living over a ridge. I did the hammering and sawing and Vange saw that the work was done right. I never was much good with my hands, even though I was trained as an engineer."

Five more long days inched by as they remained in the miserable limbo of not knowing their future. The North Vietnamese came back again to check, but gave no hint they would be released.

They had just finished a scanty evening meal of rice and thin slices of boiled iguana when a clap of thunder echoed across the mountainside. "We'll be hearing more of that from now on," Hank said. "The rainy season will be starting soon. It's bad enough when you have shelter. Out here—I don't know what we'll do."

Mike was lost in reminiscing. "If this is the tenth," he mused, "I got out of the Marines nine years ago today."

"Where'd you spend your time?" Hank asked.

"Japan. I really learned to like Japanese food. Back in Portland I used to eat at a Japanese restaurant called Bush Gardens. It's on Fourth Avenue, across from Old Multnomah Hotel. Ever been there, Hank?"

"I know the location, but I've never eaten there."

"Yummmm. You oughta try their deep pan-fried prawns. And they have a cucumber salad with seafood. Mmmm. Couple of nights ago I dreamed I was sitting on a soft cushion in one of their little private rooms. I was just about to taste a prawn, when—"

"You woke up," Betty said.

"How'd you know?"

"It happened to me that way. I dreamed about a place in Chicago called The Pit where I used to go. I had a charcoal hamburger all the way up to my mouth. I was sinking my teeth in. I could taste the juice—when somebody pulled on my chain."

"That must have been me," Hank laughed. "I was trying to get a bite of a fruit salad Vange makes so well."

"What restaurants did you take Vange to in Portland?" Mike asked.

Hank dropped his face. "I didn't. She was there just a few days before we left for Asia. Then on our furlough in '63 and '64, we had a little apartment in Bloomington, Indiana, where I was working on my master's. We traveled quite a bit, but our budget never let us go above McDonald's. We must have eaten a thousand of his hamburgers one summer."

"Well, I'd settle for one just now," Betty drooled.

"Have you ever taken Vange to a fancy place?" Mike asked.

Hank slowly shook his head. Regret was reflected in his sad blue eyes.

"You have a furlough coming up, don't you?"

"Next year—if we get out."

Mike grinned. "Then first thing you do when you go back to Portland is call Bush Gardens for a reservation."

"Vange will love that," the big man sighed. "If we get out."

"Why so pessimistic?" Betty queried.

"Pass me your Bible."

Hank took the soggy, mildewed lump of paper. He carefully turned to 1 Peter 4, and read verses 12 and 13:

> *Beloved, think it not strange concerning the fiery trial which is to try you, as though some strange thing happened unto you: But rejoice, inasmuch as ye are partakers of Christ's sufferings; that, when his glory shall be revealed, ye may be glad also with exceeding joy.*

"By receiving Christ, we have become identified with him, right? That means we are partakers of his sufferings. I don't know what all these verses mean, but I think Peter is saying we Christians shouldn't think suffering unusual, because Christ suffered. Until this experience, I've never suffered much. Oh, it was a blow when my dad died from a fall. And my heart ached every time one of our kids was seriously ill. I had that kidney stone attack three years ago. That's almost more than a man can bear. I just can't keep from crying out when the pains hit. But they go away. And I can put up with the bad food, the itching, and even these chains. The ache of being away from my loved ones, the torment of not knowing whether I'll ever see them again—that's suffering.

"I was quite confident back in Happy Valley that they'd let us go. But now I don't know what's ahead. I still believe the Lord could deliver us. But that may not be his will. We have to accept it if it isn't."

"You're right, Hank," Betty reluctantly agreed. "We must accept, even desire his will at whatever cost. And I do, though sometimes I'm a little slow at seeing it his way. Five years ago I wouldn't have felt this way. I wasn't even sure I wanted to keep on living, I was so disappointed in my Christian life. I came to a crisis and the Lord used a counselor to show me that I really had to want God's best. I didn't dream then that his best would include this.

"Last year I finished all my language studies," the young woman continued. "I qualified as a senior missionary, meaning I could vote in mission conferences. I was just getting to where I could help some of the Radê young people with their problems."

"I understand," Hank said kindly. "I'd felt my real work was just about to begin when we were captured. Do you know that I had only one native convert in ten years?"

"Tang?" Betty asked.

"Yes. I'd been trying to show him the way for years. Last August he told me he'd come to a fork in the road and had taken God's way. He was baptized with some of the Radês Christmas Day. Before we were captured, the Lord had impressed me to spend more time with him, helping him get established in the Scripture."

"Maybe the Lord has a great work for Tang to do," Betty volunteered.

"I've been thinking that might be the case."

Hank stopped, suddenly aware that he had interrupted Betty, then asked, "What were your plans for this year?"

46 NO TIME FOR TOMBSTONES

"I was going to take my first furlough and go home by way of Africa and see my dad and stepmother. I have an eleven-year-old brother and six-year-old twin brother and sister. The last time I was there—that was before I surrendered my rebellious heart to the Lord—I was such a stinker the missionaries asked me to leave."

Mike had been sitting quietly without expression. Now his eyebrows lifted. "I can't imagine that."

"Oh, you didn't know the old Betty," she laughed. "Then I was planning to fly to Chicago where my sister Marilyn and some of my closest friends live. But I guess those reservations will have to be cancelled."

Mike lay down and covered his eyes with his hands.

Betty and Hank sat quietly on opposite sides of their friend and watched the black cloud swelling over the western horizon. After a few minutes, Hank got up and leaned against a tree. He was careful not to arouse the suspicions of the day guards whose eyes followed every move of the Americans.

Betty turned and looked tenderly at Mike. They were less than a year apart in age and practically the same height. Their differences had narrowed during the past two months. Her respect for his courage and loyalty had grown immeasurably, and she felt that his regard for her had risen. Hank seemed more like a father, perhaps because he was fifteen years older and the more serious of the two. Mike was becoming the brother she'd never known.

She shooed a fly from Mike's nose and saw that he was perspiring. But the weather was cool. Concerned, she put a hand to his forehead. He was burning hot.

She called Hank. "Dengue again?" he asked with concern.

"Could be. More likely, he's coming down with malaria."

When Mike awoke his speech was blurred and incoherent. His fever was down, but he was suffering violent chills. He had diarrhea and had to be assisted back and forth to the dung hole.

The next day he was delirious and complained of fading

vision. Betty begged the Viet Cong guards for quinine, aspirin, anything. They refused.

The North Vietnamese came again. Captain Son looked at Mike indifferently.

"Don't you see he has malaria? He may die without help."

"Let him die," the officer said coldly. "He is of no value to us."

The next morning the North Vietnamese left.

Betty and Hank stayed close to Mike. Hank spent much of the time praying. Betty bathed Mike's face and kept pleading with him to eat and drink. Without nourishment, she knew he would soon die from dehydration.

"Please, please, if you have any mercy," she cried to the guards. "Help him."

They did nothing.

"At least let Pastor Ngue come and pray for him."

They called Ngue over. "What difference will it make?" the head guard grunted.

The preacher prayed. Hank and Betty couldn't be sure Mike had even heard. One minute he was raving, the next snoring.

That night he talked out of his head a long time. He was directing a crew of Radês in building a fish pond. Explaining how to operate a tractor. Planning how the tribespeople could make a profit by selling handmade articles in the craft shop he'd set up beside the Radê church.

The next morning Ngue was allowed to pray again. He lingered to whisper to Betty, "I overheard two guards talking in a Mnong dialect. They didn't think I understood. I am to be killed in four days."

"They wouldn't—"

"Yes, *Amai* Betty, they will. Three friends and I are going to try and escape. We will tell the Special Forces to come and rescue you."

"You must not hurt anyone," Betty cautioned.

"We will not do that. I promise."

That evening while Mike lay in semiconsciousness, Betty and Hank heard the whistling of a familiar tune. The whistler was standing with his back to them, fifty or sixty feet away. They could only make out his shape, but they knew it was Ngue. They followed the song in their memories:

> *God be with you till we meet again;*
> *By His counsels guide, uphold you,*
> *With His sheep securely fold you;*
> *God be with you till we meet again.*
> *Till we meet ... till we meet,*
> *Till we meet at Jesus' feet;*
> *Till we meet ... till we meet,*
> *God be with you till we meet again.*

Their beloved friend was telling them goodbye.

Betty casually strolled into the clearing. A few yards from Ngue she turned and faced away from him so the guards wouldn't think they were communicating.

"Take me with you, Pastor. Please take me with you," she blurted. She was so young and pitiful with tears coursing down her cheeks that Ngue felt his heart would break.

"I can't, *Amai*. If I had the strength I would gladly carry you on my back to safety, but we would never make it. I would be taking you to certain death."

"I—I don't know how much longer I can take this, Pastor. Couldn't I just try? If I fell behind, you could just leave me," she sobbed wiping her tears on her sleeve.

"No, the terrain is too rough and you are too weak," he explained. By this time he was crying too. "The best thing I can do is go for help. You know I will come back for you, don't you?"

"Yes, I know. But it's so hard."

"Besides, Mike is very sick. He needs you."

"Yes. That's right. Mike needs me. Very well. We'll wait for you."

"Pray for me," Ngue whispered as a guard started toward him. He went back to his hut, and Betty returned to Mike and Hank to report what had been said.

Ngue and his fellow tribesmen waited until about two hours before dawn. Then, when the patrol passed their sleeping mats, they arose quietly. They tiptoed along behind the guards, a few paces back, until they passed through the thick woods at the edge of the camp. At this point, they took off running. By the time the patrol realized what had happened, the Radês had melted into the jungle.

Betty and Hank were roused by the shouting and yelling. It quickly became clear that Ngue and some companions had made their break. As armed Viet Cong ran into the woods in blind pursuit, the missionaries prayed fervently that the Radês would be successful.

Several hours later the searchers returned. Flushed and frowning, they told their American captives nothing. Betty was confident. "If they'd caught them, they'd be bragging. Ngue will get home and bring help. I know he will."

Betty and Hank had no doubts that Ngue and his friends had gotten away when the Viet Cong broke camp and packed to move. The missionaries got Mike to his feet and helped him walk; otherwise the Communist guerrillas would have left him to die. Fortunately for Mike, they didn't go far this time. They made camp on a level spot on the bank of a cool, flowing stream.

Here Mike seemed only to get worse. His hair turned white and began falling out. For several days he was completely blind. Hour after hour, Betty kept watch beside him, forcing him to eat and drink, wrapping his blanket tight when he was chilled, cooling his face with water carried from the stream in bamboo tubes when he perspired. The only attention his guards gave was to add salt and sometimes sugar to his rice gruel.

Betty sang hymns and Hank quoted Scripture. When the guards were out of earshot she whispered of Ngue's escape. "He won't abandon us," she assured. "If he's still alive, he'll get help. I know he will. Come on, Mike. You have to eat and get your strength back for when they come to rescue us."

CHAPTER 5

Prisoners on Display

The North Vietnamese came for a check and ordered camp to be moved again. With Hank supporting Mike, and Betty staggering behind, the prisoners somehow managed to keep up during the half-day's walk in the suffocating heat and humidity. They stopped again for a week or ten days, then moved on another half day. The position of the sun indicated they had turned south into Tuyen Duc Province.

At times Mike seemed more dead than alive as he battled with malaria. Sitting beside him, Betty and Hank fought to keep him conscious; they were afraid he might lapse into a coma and die.

When he would start to pass out, Betty would slap him, shake him awake, anything to arouse him to consciousness.

When he would protest, "I'm not hungry," as he frequently did, she would press the bowl of rice gruel to his feverish lips and say, "You must eat, Mike. You can't give up now. We're depending on you."

Two weeks passed and he was still alive. Three weeks. Four. He wasn't a complainer and Betty had to drag the symptoms out of him. One symptom was obvious. He would be sitting, chained to a tree or to Hank or Betty, when everything would suddenly turn a blinding white. He'd hear a whoosh in his ears and fall over, remaining unconscious for several hours. Then a short time later he would be stricken again by the same frightening whiteness.

Mike was most talkative when delirious. One night he took them fishing for salmon in a cold, clear tributary of the Columbia River. Another evening he raced his copper sorrel horse, Satan, around the rim of a canyon.

He called the names of his mother, stepfather, sister Lynn, and boyhood friends who were unknown to Betty and Hank. He led yells for his high school basketball team, gave speeches about the customs of the tribespeople of Viet Nam, pled with superior officers for cement and building materials to start a new project. And he had words for their captors in his delirium: "Give me back my Radê bracelet and watch. Return the money you took from the lady. Free us."

On the thirty-fifth day his temperature dropped back to normal. He could see, though bright sunlight hurt his eyes. He could walk a few steps without stumbling. He even had an appetite for the unappealing food.

He asked about Ngue. "The preacher escaped, Mike," Hank said. "Don't you remember? They went looking for him and I don't think they caught him and his friends."

"Maybe he'll bring back a rescue party."

Betty forced a weak smile. "Hank and I have been praying and hoping. But they've moved us so many times. And we're 'way south of where he left us. I wonder if anyone can find us now."

The three captives looked at each other. Mike was thin and gaunt, forty or fifty pounds lighter than when they had left Happy Valley. Hank's cheeks were hollow, his blue eyes bulging in their sockets, his shoulder blades ridging the thin, short-sleeved shirt that fell loosely around thin arms. Betty's red hair, which she'd always kept bright and shiny, lay dull and straight against a scalp infested with lice. Her once pretty face was pale and pallid, with sunken cheekbones and sagging chin.

They tottered about on limbs that looked more like piano legs. Their stomachs were enlarged and distended, bloated not from food but from gas in the intestines.

Their captors began moving again, stopping for a week or two at temporary camp sites, turning southwest and remaining in the mountains. They saw occasional bands of Viet Cong, but only passed through burned-out villages from which the inhabitants had long since fled.

It was a scavenger's existence even for their Viet Cong guards, who subsisted on the same diet as the prisoners. However, it seemed Mike could eat anything. He caught lizards on rocks, small crabs in streams, and tree frogs which constantly chirped in chorus along the trails. When it wasn't convenient to boil them, he popped the frogs into his mouth and swallowed them alive.

The monsoons caught up with them in June after—according to Mike's guess—they moved into Lamdong Province, some hundred miles due south of Banmethuot. He estimated they'd walked in a roundabout, zigzag way, more than 200 miles across some of the roughest terrain in Asia.

They camped in a green depression on the side of a steep mountain and the remaining tribal prisoners were put to work cutting poles and making thatch for houses. The Americans figured this was a sign they would remain here a while.

A swift stream ran a hundred yards or so below them. Between the camp and the stream was a cave. Mike, Betty, and Hank felt this was the best place to go for shelter from the torrential rains, but the Viet Cong guards said no, and gave them a strip of plastic for a temporary roof over their heads.

When finished, the pole houses were not effective against the rain. The three again asked to go to the cave, and again were forbidden.

The skies cleared later in the evening and a luminous moon climbed into the quiet night sky. The captives were too exhausted to enjoy the beauty.

Around noon the next day, visitors arrived.

These North Vietnamese were unusually friendly. The leader, Major Phu, told the prisoners they would no longer be chained at night. "You will have the freedom of the camp, so long as you do not try anything foolish," he said.

Betty laughed ruefully, saying, "We're too weak to go far, even if we could get away."

This officer inquired about their families. Upon learning that Hank had a wife and four children, he invited Hank to write Vange. "Tell her you've been treated well and I'll deliver it to a post office myself," he promised.

Hank gratefully took a pad of paper and a pencil from Major Phu. Taking advantage of rare midday sunshine, he stretched forward on a mossy rock to write.

He wrote as positively as he could, believing that the letter would not be delivered otherwise.

He requested that she pass word to Betty's and Mike's families that they were doing as well as could be expected. Then he asked about each of the children and expressed his hope that Cindy was now with them. "I hope that the National Liberation Front will be merciful and permit me to be reunited with you soon," he added.

"This is a beautiful spot where we are now camped," he continued. "I can't name all the different butterflies I've seen. The Monarchs and Birdwings are huge! Perhaps one day we can come here and catch some for your collection."

Then he signed, "Your loving husband" and his name, and carefully slid the folded note into the envelope Major Phu

SOUTH VIET NAM

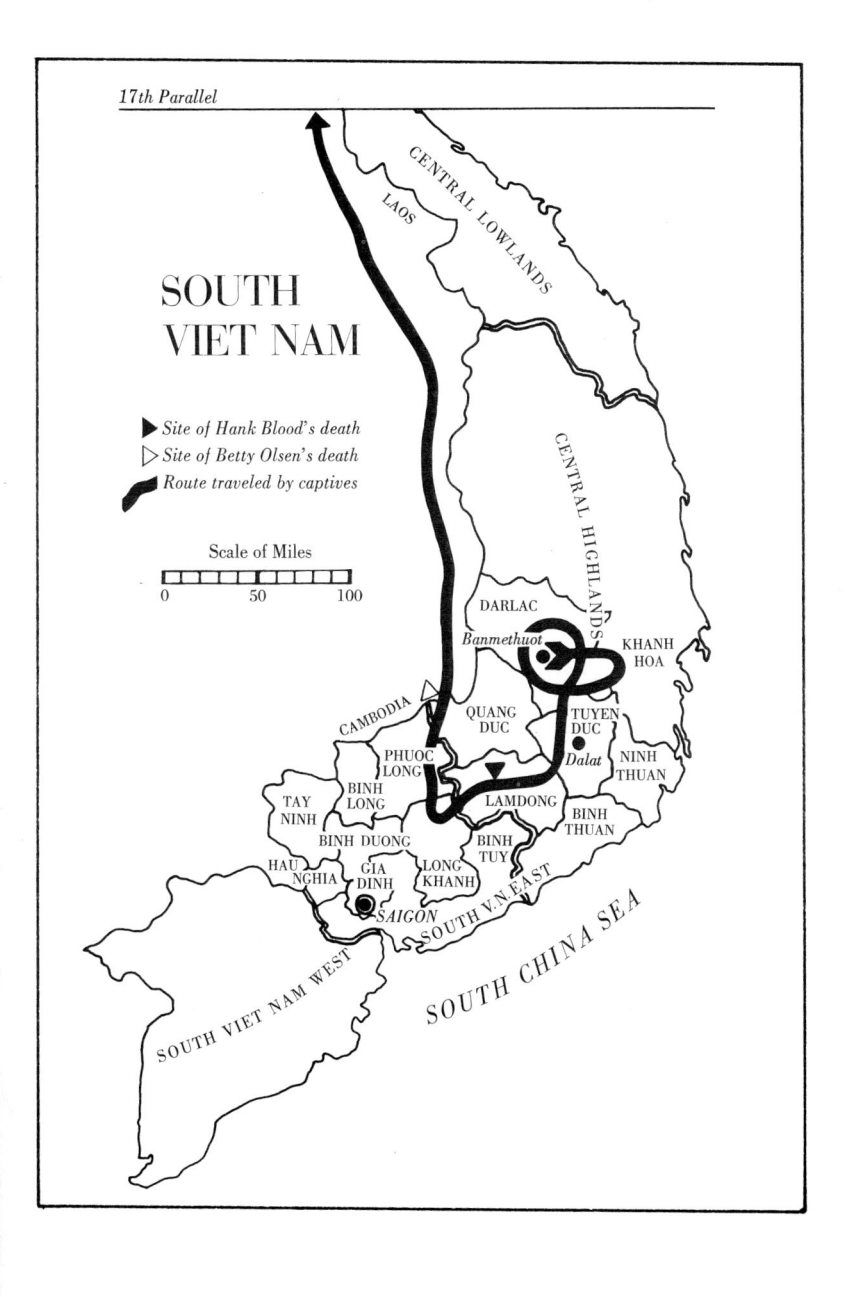

▶ *Site of Hank Blood's death*
▷ *Site of Betty Olsen's death*
━ *Route traveled by captives*

Scale of Miles
0 — 50 — 100

17th Parallel

LAOS
CENTRAL LOWLANDS
CENTRAL HIGHLANDS
CAMBODIA
DARLAC
Banmethuot
KHANH HOA
QUANG DUC
TUYEN DUC
Dalat
NINH THUAN
PHUOC LONG
LAMDONG
BINH THUAN
TAY NINH
BINH LONG
BINH DUONG
BINH TUY
LONG KHANH
HAU NGHIA
GIA DINH
SAIGON
SOUTH V.N. EAST
SOUTH VIET NAM WEST
SOUTH CHINA SEA

▲ The Radês, like some American Indian tribes, "bury" their dead above ground.
▼ Eager to be one with the tribespeople, Mike Benge often made his home in this kind of village longhouse. Here a Radê woman stands beside the horns of a water buffalo sacrificed to the spirits.

◀ *Hank Blood in his bachelor days.*
▶ *A honeymoon view of Hank and Vange Blood in the Philippines.*
▼ *This rented house was home for the Bloods at the time of Hank's capture.*

▲ A page from Hank's notebook expresses a thought which proved to be prophetic.
▼ These were among the Scripture memory cards carried by Hank during his captivity.

▲ *Cindy Blood celebrates her first birthday with an elephant ride.*
▼ *Hank and Vange with Cindy, David, and Carolyn. Cathy later completed the family.*

Personal Disciplines of Love

1. Rom 14:7 "Don't live to myself"
   I Cor 8, 10
2. Eph 5:16 "I will make the best use of my time"
3. Matt 18:15 ① I will follow
   Matt 5:24 scripture when disharmony arises.
   ② If bring gift & there is ought correct it first"
4. I Pet 2:23 — I will expect many opportunities to be accused falsely
5. Rom 13 — Cheerfully accept every responsibility as from the Lord
6. Heb 10:24 I will seek to build God's word in lives of others

These notes came out of Betty's life-changing counseling sessions with Bill Gothard.

◀ *Betty earned her coveted nurse's cap at Methodist Hospital in Brooklyn.*
▶ *Betty Olsen at age 9 and her sister Marilyn, 6, with their parents, Rev. and Mrs. Walter Olsen.*
▼ *A love of outdoor life—good preparation for Betty's service in Viet Nam.*

In memory of those
valiant missionaries who
here laid down their lives
during tet. 1968 —

NATHAN ROBERT ZIEMER
CARL EDWARD THOMPSON
RUTH STEBBINS THOMPSON
LEON C. GRISWOLD
CAROLYN RUTH GRISWOLD
RUTH MARGARET WILTING

This beautiful memorial at Banmethuot marks the graves of some of those who died in the Tet massacre.

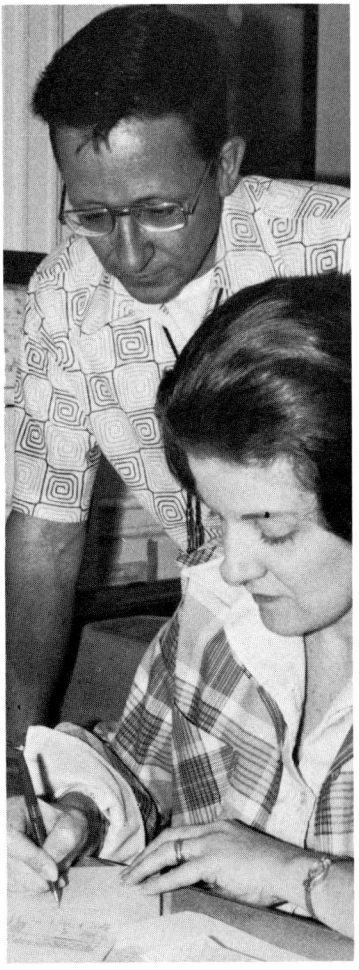

◀ *Back on U.S. soil, Mike recuperates from his long ordeal as a captive of the North Vietnamese. Author James Hefley took these photos during the interviews in which Mike shared the painful memories which form the basis for this book.*
▶ *Mike in Corpus Christi, Texas, to address rally for M.I.A. (Missing in Action) families. Here he dictates a letter to Sandy Olsen, leader of the Corpus Christi M.I.A. chapter.*

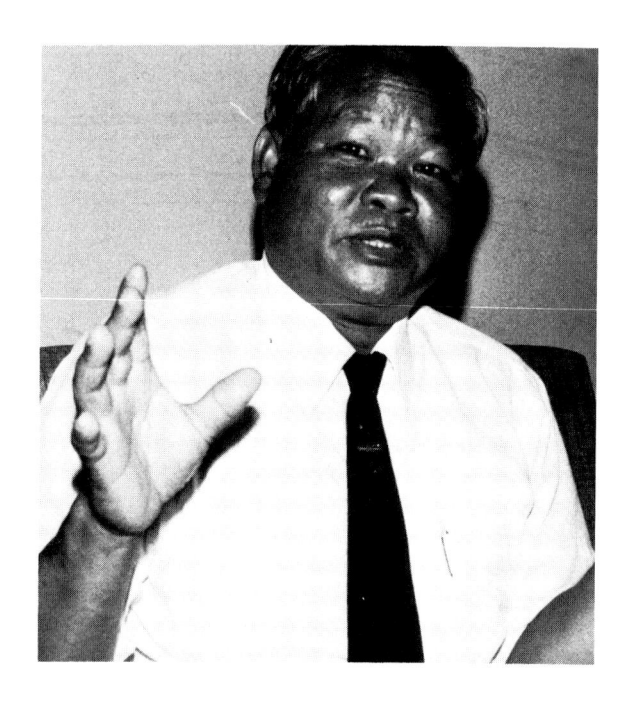

Pastor Ngue was captured with Hank, Betty, and Mike, but was able to escape and find his way back home through the jungle. Ngue is now district superintendent of the tribal churches.

Hank with Tang, his only tribal convert in Viet Nam. Tang has become a leading evangelist, winning many to Christ.

▲ Banmethuot tribal Bible school was reopened shortly after Tet offensive. All the destroyed mission homes and buildings there have been rebuilt and a great tribal revival has taken place.
▼ The American troops are gone, but Alliance missionaries continue to serve Christ in cooperation with the National Evangelical Church. This literature truck in Saigon is one means of outreach.

had given him. The officer took the letter and again pledged that Vange would get it. Hank told his companions, "I believe he is sincere."

The attempted correspondence seemed to make Hank long even more for his wife and children. He felt that Vange and the three youngest had certainly been allowed to go ahead to safety. He could not be so sure about Cindy, the oldest. Mike had said that before his ill-fated rescue attempt, he'd heard that the attack on Banmethuot was part of a country-wide North Vietnamese and Viet Cong offensive.

Hank, Betty, and Mike had frequently speculated about what might have happened at Kontum, which was some 140 miles north of Banmethuot. Eleven Wycliffe members and two Alliance couples had been there participating in a translation workshop.

"We know the 173rd Airborne pulled out just before *Tet*," Hank mentioned again. "With them gone, the enemy might have taken Kontum. Nobody in the camps has given us any information. We just don't know. I sure do hope Cindy wasn't hurt. Poor little thing, barely nine years old, up there at school, away from her family."

"She may have been better off there than if she'd been at Banmethuot," Betty mused.

"Yes, I've thought of that. And I've surrendered her to the Lord's keeping. But I can't keep her out of my mind.

"I remember her first birthday. We put her on an elephant and I took pictures. Wish I had one to show you how cute and tiny she looked on that huge beast. Vange and I thought she was really the cat's whiskers.

"Mike, you and Betty will just never understand how it is 'till you marry and have children yourselves. One of the toughest things about being a missionary is sending your children away to school."

"Remember, I'm a missionary kid myself, Hank," Betty reminded. "I don't know how many times I cried myself to sleep, wishing I could see my parents."

Hank turned his face so Mike and Betty couldn't see his tears. But they could see his bony shoulders shaking and hear the sobs.

"I'm sorry, Hank," Betty said gently. "I didn't mean—"

"I know you didn't, Betty," Hank cried. "It's just that I miss them so much. O God, if I could hold each of them just once more. Just to tell them how much I love them. It hurts. Oh, how it hurts."

Mike and Betty sat silent, trying to sympathize, but not knowing what to say.

After a while they heard Hank blow his nose in some leaves. Then he turned back to face them. The tears had dried on his face.

"The Lord's watching over them. I know he is. He watched over them in the past. He will now.

"I remember when we were on furlough and I was studying for my master's at Indiana. I came home from conference and found little Carolyn—she was just a tiny baby—looking like a chalk doll. Vange said she'd lost weight. Well, she didn't have much to lose. The doctor told us she was critical and might die. He wanted to operate.

"That evening I dug into the Word. I read about Abraham and Paul—men who dared to believe that God would work miracles. After an hour and a half of Bible study and prayer, I committed her to the Lord and slept soundly.

"We took her to Indianapolis and the doctors operated. They found her diaphragm had ruptured and her intestines were pushing up into the lung cavity and crowding the lungs and heart. They fixed her diaphragm and pushed the intestines back to where they belonged. Fifteen days later she was out of the hospital and we could hardly tell she'd been sick. Some said we were lucky to have her alive, but we knew it was the Lord who helped the doctors do what they did.

"I can point to so many times when the Lord seemed to be looking after the Blood family," Hank continued. "Back in '62 Vange and I went to Saigon for medical checkups. One of our group members had tried to make an appointment, but the nurses had said we didn't need it and should just come on in. Apparently there was a mix-up, for when we went to see the doctor, he said we had to have an appointment. That made it necessary to cancel our flight reservations.

"When we got back to Banmethuot I checked with the government security office about going on out to Lac Thien. He said we couldn't because there had been an attack the night before and the VC flag was flying over the town. If we had gone as originally scheduled, we probably would have been captured. We were saved by a misunderstanding.

"This was in March. A couple of months later we got the children ready to go see Dr. Vietti at the leprosarium. She delivered David, you know. We had planned to go earlier, but it was the 30th before we were packed up. Then someone told us to forget it, because the night before, the doctor, Dan Gerber, and Archie Mitchell had been captured. So it seemed the Lord was looking out for us again.

"But we were in the right spot this time and they got me. I don't know why the Lord has permitted this to happen, but I'm sure he has a purpose. 'All things work together for good to those that love God.' He knows what's best."

"Yes," Betty murmured. "Bad as it is, we have to believe that the Lord has reasons we don't understand."

"Yes," Hank said. "And instead of sitting here thinking about the greatness of our predicament, we should be thinking about the greatness of God. He has his eye on the world and all the things that are happening to his children. He's listening to our prayers and the prayers of others, even if he doesn't answer as we'd like him to.

"When I think of all the people who must be praying for us," he added, "I know he must have something for us to do here. Why, my mother probably has half the people in Oregon praying."

"How old is she now, Hank?" Mike asked.

"Eighty-one."

"She's certainly spry. I saw her at the dedication of your Translation Center in Kontum three years ago."

"I'd planned to be there, but my kidneys acted up and we had to extend our furlough in the States. She got to see Dave and Doris and their little son, Jeffrey. She went all the way up to Quang Tri where Carolyn and John Miller were working with the Bru. My mom is some gal, all right."

Calmer and less emotional now, Hank kept talking about his family. "Dave and I couldn't have had better parents. I remember when Dad was living, we'd pack up and go on camping trips. Cannon Beach. On the slopes of Mt. Hood. We'd take the road up the Columbia River, then loop back the long way around Mt. Hood. I guess you've been that route, Mike."

"Sure thing. Boy, I'd love to stand under Bridal Veil Falls and feel the sweet sting of spray on my face. That's one of the coolest places on earth. Then I'd like to stop at a roadside restaurant and have about a pound of bacon and a dozen fresh eggs. With some good hot coffee."

"I always thought I couldn't get by without my coffee in the morning," Betty said. "My sister Marilyn even sent me a thermos so I could have a hot cup waiting when I woke up each morning. I could drink a thermos full right now."

Hank licked his lips. "I'd settle for a half gallon of vanilla ice cream. When Dave and I were kids, Mom would treat the whole neighborhood. Drool!"

"Well, shall we order now?" Mike joked. " 'Hey, waiter, I'll have a dozen eggs, over easy, with a big side order of bacon. And six pieces of hot toast.' What'll you have for your main course, Betty?"

"With my coffee, I'd like some *duos*. That's a big African potato. Boiled, mashed, or baked. I don't care. And a bowl of peanut soup."

"And you, Mr. Blood. What's your preference on the menu?"

"Three McDonald doubleburgers. A pound of fries. And a

gallon of vanilla ice cream. Tell the cooks to hurry. I'm starved."

The three sat cross-legged, pretending to enjoy their imaginary food.

Betty giggled—the first time in days. "The guards think we're crazy."

"Oh, they've thought that all along," Hank said. "Maybe they'll send us to a mental institution where the food is better than here."

"Shhhh," Mike whispered. "Don't tell anyone, but we're in one already."

"Oh, Mike, what would we do without your sense of humor?"

"Where? What? I lost it the first day of *Tet*."

After a while they grew tired of pretending and Betty told her Bible story for the day. This one was about Queen Esther, who saved the Jewish people from mass murder.

When she concluded, Mike asked curiously, "Do the good people always win out in the Bible?"

"If you mean do they always turn out to be healthy, wealthy, and wise—no. Stephen was stoned to death. The Apostle Paul probably died in prison or had his head chopped off by the Emperor Nero."

"I remember reading," Hank put in, "that there's pretty good evidence for every one of Jesus' twelve apostles dying a violent death. Except the Apostle John, who died in Ephesus, after his exile on the island of Patmos."

After a while they lay down to nap. Mike was just dozing off when he smelled corn cooking. Someone had brought in a new supply of vegetables.

He told Hank and Betty and they waited expectantly for a little variety in the evening meal. They were served nothing but thin rice.

Stomachs aching, mouths watering, they sat licking their bowls, hungry eyes on the guards who were slurping corn and squash by the fire a few feet away.

"May we have some of the new food?" Betty finally asked.

The guards looked at the three starving Americans and laughed. Then one said, "You may search the ashes when we're done."

The three captives were desperate. They were not too proud to do that. As soon as the ashes cooled they groped on their knees for grains of corn. "Now I know how Lazarus felt," Hank said.

North Vietnamese officers came by again. The Americans were always glad to see them. When they came, food rations improved. And there remained the flicker of hope that this might be the time of release. Since the capture at Banmethuot, NVAs had always stayed in the area, maintaining regular checks on the rag-tag Viet Cong.

These new officers were polite but curt. They listened to their pleas, as had previous NVA visitors. They, as had the others, scoffed at the idea that Americans could be in Viet Nam for purely altruistic reasons. And they rebuffed Hank's usual efforts to talk to them about God and the Bible.

When the captain informed the prisoners they were going to "take a little walk," they groaned. None of them was in any condition for another hike. They were so weak from the effects of malnutrition they didn't see how they could walk a hundred yards.

"Could they be turning us loose?" Betty asked hopefully. The thought spurred the trio to try. They staggered along through the insect-infected jungle, trying to support one another as best they could. Only the leeches enjoyed the hike. They were so numerous that the marchers had to stop often to pull them loose.

It took them half a day to get to the other side of the mountain, where they stumbled into the camp of a regiment of NVA troops.

These soldiers were well fed and appeared to be in good health. The prisoners gaped at several crates of medicine stacked in a tent. Betty begged for sulfa, quinine, penicillin, anything they could spare. She was ignored.

Their escort marched them in front of the soldiers like cattle at an auction.

"What's he going to do with us?" Betty whispered to her male companions who stood protectively on either side of her.

"Maybe we'll get medals," Mike replied wryly.

The regiment commander spoke in Vietnamese, which all three understood.

"Comrades, we have brought from the prison camp three imperialist spies from America, Mr. Michael Benge, Mr. Henry Blood, and Miss Betty Olsen. We do not know why the pretty lady is without a husband. Perhaps she will tell us."

The troops guffawed.

"We have told you that Americans are accustomed to a soft life of ease and luxury. This is because they exploit poor and struggling peoples who do not yet understand the aims of our glorious socialist revolution. Americans walk very little. They ride in limousines and airplanes.

"These imperialist plotters have round stomachs and small legs because of lack of exercise. This is how you would look if you traveled as they do."

The subjects of the demonstration were grinding their teeth in frustration. If the poor dupes only knew... Finally Mike could stand it no longer. "You fools!" he screamed in Vietnamese. "Can't you see that we look this way because your comrades are starving us to death!"

The Captain's hand lashed out with a stinging blow to Mike's jaw that sent him reeling. "You are bad, Mr. Benge," he hissed through his teeth. "Very bad. You will regret those remarks!"

CHAPTER 6

Sorrow on the Mountain

"The presence of you imperialist spies contaminates our brave fighting men," the officer shouted for all to hear. He ordered the three Americans taken back to their prison camp immediately.

"Move! Move!" their escorts shouted as they stumbled along the precipitous trail. Mike was so dizzy he could hardly stand. Betty's bare legs burned and bled from the bloodlusting leaches that clung to her. The angry North Vietnamese would not permit her to slow down long enough to pull them off. Hank wobbled in uncertain agony. The pain from the huge boil on his hip was excruciating. Ugly ulcers were breaking out on his arms. The odor from the ulcers smelled to his companions like burned beans. "Please stop, please!" he begged, to no avail.

The trip seemed endless. Besides their physical condition, the hopelessness of their situation was an added burden that weighed heavily on their hearts.

When they finally reached the little hut that was their prison cell they collapsed on the straw mats. They looked more dead than alive. Betty clawed at the leeches. Mike tried to help her, but kept falling back as his head whirled. Hank groaned, trying not to move.

Mercifully, the North Vietnamese left them alone for a while.

After an hour or two they started down hill to the stream. Betty went first, slipping and sliding, with Mike, still dizzy, hanging onto her hand. Hank inched painfully along behind them.

They stayed as long as they dared, washing their bodies, picking lice from one another's heads, rejuvenating their tortured minds with the sound of water gently gurgling over mossy rocks. "If we could only shut our eyes and be in Oregon," Hank sighed. "The streams are like this there."

"Americans! Come!"

The voice was insistent. They had never been physically assaulted in any camp, but the tone suggested this was now a possibility.

Climbing back up was torture. They made it to the cave on the side of the hill when Hank collapsed and said, "I can't go any farther."

Mike and Betty tried to help, but didn't have the strength to pull his body forward more than a few feet. They went on alone, gasping, supporting one another, half dragging their bodies until they reached the camp.

"Mr. Blood is too weak," Mike panted. "He must have assistance."

One of the North Vietnamese motioned to two tribal prisoners to go bring Hank up. When this was accomplished, an NVA officer herded the three captives together for interrogation.

"When will you admit that you are spies?" he demanded.

"When will you believe that we are here because we want to help the tribespeople?" Mike responded. "The lady is a volunteer nurse with the lepers. Mr. Blood is a Bible teacher. I am an agricultural technician."

This NVA, who had never given his name, slammed the butt of his rifle against the ground. "Ridiculous!"

He looked at Betty, huddled on the ground, trying to preserve as much modesty as her thin dress would allow. "Since you are a woman, perhaps the National Liberation Front will be lenient if you tell the truth."

Betty looked deep into the accuser's eyes. "Captain, we have always told the truth to every officer who has questioned us. No one would believe us."

"You are lying, Miss Olsen. No American would come here for humanitarianism."

"I believe you are sincere, Captain," Betty sighed weakly. "But Communism won't satisfy the deepest longings of your heart. Don't you wonder sometimes what life is all about, why you are here, where you are going when you die?"

"Man dies like all other animals. There is nothing more."

"That's what you have been taught. But man is eternal. When he dies, he goes to heaven or hell."

"Ha! That is just American imperialist propaganda. Karl Marx said religion is the opiate of the people. It makes people afraid by persuading them to believe in superstitions. Then your imperialist profiteers attach their greedy tentacles. We are going to change all that."

"Captain, we cannot persuade you. Only God can do that. We can only pray for you."

Hank had revived enough to join in the discussion. "Captain," he asked, "do you say Christianity is a tool of the West?"

"Yes. It is ammunition in the arsenal of the capitalists of Wall Street."

"Captain, history tells us that Christianity began in the

Middle East and spread first through those lands and into Europe and Asia. Jesus Christ lived centuries before Karl Marx and Ho Chi Minh."

"Jesus Christ is dead."

"He died, but did not stay dead. He rose from the grave the third day. He lives in the hearts of all those who believe in him and love him. He lives in our hearts. That is why we've come to Viet Nam. We're here as his representatives."

"Enough!" the NVA suddenly shouted. "We have more important work to do than debate such foolishness. You are either spies, or you are stupid."

"If we are stupid, we can harm no one," Mike suggested. "Why not let us go?"

The NVA didn't reply.

"Well, we tried again," Betty sighed after the NVA and his fellow officers had left.

"Don't be discouraged, Betty," Hank consoled. "If we are faithful in witnessing, God will tend to the results."

Hank shifted his body, grimacing in pain. "The devil wants to knock us out of battle. The Lord wants us to depend completely on him. Every day since we were captured, I've told him, 'Here is my life. I belong to you. Give me the right sense of perspective.'

"It hasn't been easy. I've wanted to give up. Quit. Lie down and die. Or smack a VC or NVA in the teeth. Then I think, they don't know what they're doing. Remember how the Lord prayed for his enemies on the cross: 'Father, forgive them, for they know not what they do.' "

Mike had sat silent for some time. Now he confessed, "That's easier said than done."

"We can, Mike," Betty declared. "With God's spirit living in us, we can."

"Yes," Hank said, quoting Matthew 5:44: " 'Love your enemies, bless them that curse you, do good to them that hate you, and pray for them which despitefully use you, and persecute you.' "

"Lord, help us keep on loving," Betty prayed. "Loving one another. Loving our enemies. Trusting you." Then in a weak, trembling voice, she led out in a stanza of a favorite hymn:

> *Simply trusting every day,*
> *Trusting through a stormy way;*
> *Even when my faith is small,*
> *Trusting Jesus, that is all.*

The next week the ugly boil on Hank's side burst and began draining. He seemed to have a harder time sleeping than ever. The sharp, sudden kidney pains kept recurring. The itching had never ceased. He moaned in his sleep and suffered frightful nightmares. Sometimes it seemed as if the Lord and the devil were battling for possession of his body.

Reduced to a thin shadow, Hank seemed to sense the future, noting, "Next month I'll be forty-nine. I wonder if I'll live that long."

The nights were chilly here on the mountain and sometimes the damp, cold air seemed to knife through the prisoners. One especially frigid night, Mike was trying to huddle near a tribal prisoner. The tribesman heard him shivering and chattering and offered to share his blanket. "It's full of lice, Mr. Benge," the Radê warned.

Mike was so cold he didn't care. "I'd rather have lice than freeze to death," he said, snuggling under it.

The next day the tribesman gave Mike the blanket, which he in turn shared with Hank and Betty. They begged their guards to let them boil this blanket and other lice-infested bedding and clothes, but the VCs coldly refused.

The food was the worst it had been. Usually they'd had manioc and occasional meat or dried fish, to supplement the monotonous bowl of rice. Now they were receiving only rice.

"We won't last much longer if you don't give us more food and some medical aid," Mike told the NVA, the next time they came around.

They appeared not to care. "You're of no political value to us," one officer shrugged. "If you die, we'll have three less problems."

Did they mean they were no longer considered spies? They could only guess.

The rainy season still had two months to run. They were getting a heavy downpour at least once a day and sometimes twice. Their VC guards wouldn't let them go to the cave, so they had to huddle in their leaky pole hut under the strip of plastic and wait each storm out. Invariably, either Mike or Hank got soaking wet. The covering was simply not adequate for three people.

The night of July 10th was a time, as Hank remarked, when old Noah would have felt right at home. The rain fell in drenching sheets, hour after dark hour. No matter how they positioned themselves, one was always exposed to the downpour. Being the longest, Hank was getting soaked the most.

"I'm going to the little house on the other side of the camp," he finally said.

"The roof leaks badly. You'll get wetter than if you stayed here," Mike warned.

"It couldn't be any worse."

"He'll catch pneumonia, Mike," Betty worried. "Weak as he is, he wouldn't last long."

The two threw off their covering and braved the rain to go bring Hank back. He returned reluctantly, soaked to the skin.

The hard rains continued into the next night. "I can't stand this," Hank complained. "I'm going to the little house. Don't come after me this time."

The next morning Mike and Betty went over to check and found Hank near pneumonia. They squeezed the water from his shirt and trouser legs and dried him off as best they could. Betty tenderly covered him up with the last dry blanket they had, while Mike summoned the head guard.

"He must have medical aid," Mike said grimly. "Can't you send a man to the military camp for medicines?"

"Those supplies are for the soldiers," the guard replied stonily. "If your troops and planes weren't here, they wouldn't need them."

"Will you let him die?" Mike declared. "Let an innocent man die? Leave four children without a father? A wife without a husband?"

"If he dies, okay. We won't be bothered. Don't worry about him. Go back to your house."

Mike and Betty would have gotten on their knees if they had thought it would help Hank. They begged and pleaded to no avail.

Finally Mike said, "Let Miss Olsen and me carry him to a hospital. We'll come back. We promise."

The Viet Cong laughed in their faces.

They could only stand watch and keep Hank as comfortable as possible.

By noon he was talking out of his head. Telling his children how to pose for pictures. Questioning a tribal informant about a Mnong legend. Leading devotions for the Wycliffe gang at Saigon. Then, in a quavering voice, trying to sing the hymn he'd chosen years before as his marching song:

> *Lead on, O King Eternal;*
> *The day of march has come;*
> *Henceforth in fields of conquest*
> *Thy tents shall be our home.*
> *Through days of preparation*
> *Thy grace has made us strong,*
> *And now, O King Eternal,*
> *We lift our battle song.*

Near the middle of the day he recognized Mike and Betty. "Has the rain stopped?" he mumbled.

Betty assured him it had.

"Let's go down to the stream and wash up." He started to rise and fell back on the blanket. "Hey, what happened? I was trying to find a dry place in here, and . . ." His voice trailed off in a dry whisper.

Betty read to him from her Bible, which by now was in such condition that she could hardly hold the sections together. Mike sat nearby, head bowed in thought and prayer.

Later in the afternoon Hank came to his senses again.

"If I don't get back, hug Vange for me, Betty. Tell her I may not be much good at building a raft, but I love her. And kiss each of my children. Cindy is big enough to understand, and maybe David. Their mother will have to tell Carolyn and Cathy when they're older why this happened.

"When you see my brother Dave, tell him he's the greatest, the best. And Mike, when you go home to Oregon, look up my mom. Give her my love. Thank her for praying for me . . .Thank . . ."

He fell back into sleep. Betty felt his forehead. "A hundred and four at least," she murmured.

He came back in a few minutes. "The Mnongs must have the Bible . . . didn't get much done . . . Vange, ask Tang to help . . . Vange . . . you're strong . . . you can do it."

Then, "Tang . . . don't forget the Bible verses you learned . . . Give your people God's Word . . . I can't . . . can't . . . please help . . .

"Betty . . . Mike, you're still here . . . Oh, how my hip hurts . . . Betty, give me a shot . . . help me . . ."

"Vange, I . . . love. Cathy . . . David . . . Carolyn . . . Cindy . . ."

The first evening stars came out in the clear sky. Hank was quieter now, snoring. But his fever was still high.

Betty saw that Mike wasn't doing so well either. She feared the malaria might be coming back, and insisted he go to bed.

She stayed beside Hank as long as she could keep her head up, then dropped into exhausted sleep. The camp lay quiet in the ve'vet Vietnamese night.

For another day and night Betty nursed Hank as much as she was able, while keeping a weary eye on Mike, who had become delirious again.

On the morning of July 13th, or perhaps the 14th, Hank had no pulse. Restraining the bitterness she felt, she called the guards and asked them to dig a grave.

They complied.

Mike was a little better. At his request, the guards gave them a couple of empty rice bags. He and Betty pulled one over Hank's head and the other over his feet.

Then the Viet Cong picked up Hank's long body and carried it to the shallow grave under the shade of a nearby tree. They stood by unsmiling as Betty recited,

> *The Lord is my shepherd; I shall not want. He maketh me to lie down in green pastures: he leadeth me beside the still waters. He restoreth my soul: he leadeth me in the paths of righteousness for his name's sake. Yea, though I walk through the valley of the shadow of death, I will fear no evil: for thou art with me; thy rod and thy staff they comfort me. Thou preparest a table before me in the presence of mine enemies: thou anointest my head with oil; my cup runneth over. Surely goodness and mercy shall follow me all the days of my life: and I will dwell in the house of the Lord forever.*

The body was in the shallow hole and they were ready to cover it. "Wait," commanded Betty in Vietnamese.

"Earth to earth, ashes to ashes, dust to dust. We commend the soul of our brother Hank to the God and Father of our Lord Jesus Christ."

A shovel crunched into the loose earth. The first shower of dirt slapped against the body. Betty clung to Mike's arm. They turned back to the camp.

CHAPTER 7

Betty's Victory

Hank's death was like a bad dream to Mike, whose fever lasted for several days afterward. Betty, despite her sores and the miserable diet, was more able to keep her senses together. When Mike felt better, he was chagrined to realize that throughout their ordeal, she had remained the healthiest.

"I've always considered myself tough," he admitted to Betty. "To have a woman show me up hurts my masculine pride."

Betty merely smiled and said, "Thank the Lord, one of us has always been able to keep going. If we should both go down—I don't know..."

They had dried fish for dinner. "The NVAs will be here tomorrow," Mike predicted. "The VCs always treat us better when they're expected."

This time it was Major Phu. He appeared to be genuinely sorry that Hank had died. "I came to tell him I mailed his letter," he said.

"How much longer are we to be held?" Betty asked.

The NVA major pleaded ignorance. He did say that since the rainy season was almost over they would be moved again.

Mike inquired—as they had all along—if he'd heard of three American missionaries, two men and a woman doctor, being in a prison camp. "They were taken six years ago," he added.

"No, I've never seen any report of this," Major Phu replied. "But we've been told that the National Liberation Front captured 500 Americans at Banmethuot."

This was news to Betty and Mike. They didn't believe it and said so. There had never been that many Americans in Banmethuot.

"What's happening in the rest of the world?" Betty asked.

"Oh, there are very bad riots in your country. The people are rising up to protest Johnson's imperialist war."

Betty and Mike didn't know how much of this to believe.

Major Phu left, and about a week later, on July 28th, their Viet Cong guards started moving them down the mountain. Though weak and emaciated, Betty and Mike tried to memorize the features of the place in hopes they might be able to return and locate Hank's grave after release.

They camped the next time in flatlands. The altitude was still high and the heat not oppressive. Mike thought he recognized the area as being part of Longkhanh Province, about halfway between Banmethuot and Saigon.

Here they had three new guards, all Radê and more friendly to the two captives who spoke their Montagnard dialect. Mike and Betty hadn't had so much food to eat since leaving Happy Valley.

They missed talkative Hank. The four-and-a-half months with him seemed like half a lifetime. His death lay heavy upon their thoughts. They dreaded having to tell Vange.

"Why did *he* have to die, and not one of us?" Mike wondered. "He had a wife and children. He was ready to do his translation."

"It does seem unfair," Betty admitted. "So many tragedies do, when you look at them from human reasoning. But God has his reasons for allowing Hank to die. Mike, do you remember the five missionaries who were killed by Auca Indians in Ecuador a few years ago? At the time it seemed so useless. Such a waste. They were all young and talented and just beginning their work. Four of them were married and there were several children involved.

"But the shock of their deaths shook a lot of American Christians. Hundreds of young people were challenged to become missionaries. Perhaps the story of what happened to Hank and to our friends back at Banmethuot will cause many more to volunteer. Jesus said, 'Except a corn of wheat fall into the ground and die, it abides alone: but if it dies, it brings forth much fruit.'

"I'm not saying that's it, but God has his reasons. There must be a higher purpose in all this. We'll just have to wait and see."

They celebrated Mike's thirty-third birthday on August 6th. Without candles or cake, they could have only an imaginary party. Betty sang to Mike and invited him to enjoy a repast from home: a Paul-Bunyan-size salmon steak with melted butter lake surrounded by mountains of mashed potatoes, roasting ears, homemade rolls, and iced tea. "Yummmmm," Mike murmured in pretended delight and patted his swollen stomach appreciatively. That night both dreamed about sitting down before luscious dinners. Then, as in past nocturnal fantasies, they woke up just as the food reached their mouths.

A few days later they heard a familiar voice. "Mr. Benge, Miss Olsen?"

It was Major Phu again.

"I've just come from seeing your friend's widow in Banmethuot. She took the news of her husband's death very sorrowfully. But she and the children are well, and she sends you greetings."

"Well, that takes care of that," Mike said after the NVA had left. "Now she knows—if he's telling the truth."

"He seemed sincere."

"But why would Vange stay in Banmethuot if 500 Americans were captured there?"

"I don't know," Betty said. "I'd think she'd go somewhere safer with the children."

With a more balanced diet that included meat and fish, Betty became more alert and, in spite of the depressing circumstances, laughed when telling of childhood incidents in the Ivory Coast of Africa.

"I wasn't a model missionary kid," she admitted. "Definitely not."

"What did you do that was so bad?" Mike teased.

"Once I let our African house boy kiss me. Our field chairman was visiting and saw us. Boy, was he upset."

Mike laughed out loud. "I can imagine."

"I had a habit of saying just what I thought. Missionary kids were supposed to be quiet and solemn and pious. Never were they to embarrass their parents. They had to be super good."

"I can't figure you any other way," Mike said.

"Oh, I was a mischievous little girl. Seriously, some of the happiest days of my life were spent in Africa. There was an old tree in the yard just right for climbing. I'd climb up to my perch and read books by the hour."

"What'd you read?"

"Anything I could get my hands on. I loved stories about nurses. Even back then I wanted to be one.

"Marilyn was three years younger. She didn't always understand, but she was sweet. Our house was one of those big old high-ceiling things with open rafters. I was supposed to protect Marilyn from the rats and lizards that ran around in our room.

"Our folks were marvelous people, but we felt they had too much to do on the mission station. Dad was a translator and spent a lot of time in his study. Mom never seemed to catch up with her work. And they were both always leaving us, it seemed, going on trips to visit the African churches. I can remember sitting and waiting, sitting and waiting for Mom to come home and play with me. I came to resent the work that took her away.

"Oh, Mike, I hope you don't get the wrong idea about missionaries. God's work has to come first with us, and it's terribly hard to divide your loyalties, especially when your family's involved. I didn't talk about this when Hank was living. I'm sure he was a good father, but I might have made him feel guilty. Now that I've turned myself over to the Lord fully, I can appreciate my folks more. We'll have to make up the time together in heaven."

Mike squinted at Betty who was sitting with her scarred legs hanging over a rock. "This turning yourself over to the Lord—you've mentioned that before. Just what do you mean?" he asked.

Betty looked at her companion, hesitating.

"If it's some deep, dark secret..."

"No, no. It's just that I've never been able to feel close to very many people, to really share myself. Until five years ago, I just couldn't get close to anyone."

"That's when it happened?"

"Yes, but to really help you understand how I was, I'll have to go 'way back. You see, when I was eight my folks sent Marilyn and me 800 miles away to school. There was no school at the station where they lived. It was either send us or leave their work.

"So except for furloughs, I was away from them eight months out of every year. And in high school I was away all year with kids whose parents were all over the world. In a situation like that, you learn not to make close friendships, because as soon as you get attached to someone, they leave.

"I suppose the seeds were already there, but high school

BETTY'S VICTORY 79

was where I really began to show my rebellion. I thought they were too strict—there were so many rules, we couldn't do anything. I was such a stinker at one school that my dad heard about it and made me write them an apology.

"Then my dear mom got cancer. I prayed for her to get well, oh, how I prayed. She was sick for about two years and died just before my seventeenth birthday. I accepted it as the Lord's will, at least I said I did. It was hard, Mike, awfully hard."

Mike could see the tears filling her eyes. He remembered how tough it had been when as a small child he'd lost his father.

"I finished high school. Then I went back to Africa for a while to be with my dad. In a couple of years he married Gene Swain, a single girl missionary. A really sweet person.

"I still wanted to be a nurse. In 1953 I came back and took my training at Methodist Hospital in Brooklyn, and then I worked there a couple of years. This was a very traumatic time for someone like me who'd always lived a protected life. I found it hard to accept people who did things I sometimes wanted to do, yet didn't approve of.

"They assigned me to the OB ward. I loved the little black-eyed Italian babies. I would baby-sit for the Jewish doctors' families. I hoped for a family of my own."

Betty was blushing. It seemed awkward for Mike to say anything, so he just waited.

"In our culture a fellow can take the initiative in seeking a life partner. A girl has to wait.

"Sure, I had dates. Not as many as I'd have liked. Some fellows I didn't like and one or two I might have liked better if they'd shown more interest.

"Also, I was thinking God wanted me to be a missionary, and that narrowed the field considerably. I wasn't very happy in my Christian experience, but the missionary thing stayed in the back of my mind.

"The marriage problem really began bugging me when I went to our Bible college at Nyack and majored in missions.

By this time I was 24, and the social pressure to get married was tremendous. It wasn't so bad the first or second years, but by the third year I could feel people beginning to wonder, 'What's wrong with Betty?' I wondered myself. Was it my looks, my personality, or what?

"I graduated in '62 and Marilyn and I spent five months with Dad and Gene in Seattle. Their little Mark was five then and adorable. And while they were in the States the twins were born. Then our family split up, as it seems missionary families are always doing, and they returned to Africa.

"This left me adrift. Marilyn was studying to be a religious education director. I was supposed to become a missionary, but I knew our Board wouldn't appoint me. I was too mixed up and confused.

"I went to Chicago with Marilyn. I didn't know why. Now I know it was the Lord. Marilyn and I drove an old turquoise Chevy and had a ball. We stopped and roasted wieners and picked up a hitchhiker. I was feeling pretty reckless.

"After a few months working at West Suburban Hospital in Chicago, I decided to visit the scene of my childhood, thinking that being in Africa might help me get my head together. But the missionaries there thought I was a bad influence on their work and made it plain that I should leave. I must have said some pretty awful things.

"So back to Chicago and nursing and the same old grind. Marriage prospects looked worse than ever. In another year I'd be 30 and a real old maid. I didn't like the way the future looked.

"I got more and more depressed about myself. Why couldn't I be a happy Christian? Why couldn't I make close friends like other people? Why did my conscience keep bothering me about things I'd asked over and over to be forgiven for? How was I ever going to be a missionary, feeling this way? Mike, I even reached the point where I contemplated suicide. I thought if this was all the Christian life had to offer, I'd be better off dead."

Betty stopped and looked straight into Mike's eyes. "You

probably thought missionaries and Christian workers didn't have problems like this?'"

Mike grinned enigmatically.

"Just hold on. I'm getting to the good part of the story.

"I was then attending Jefferson Park Bible Church on the north side of Chicago. There was a fellow named Bill Gothard who came around on Wednesday nights to talk with young people. He had personal conferences with each one in the youth group. I saw how much he'd helped them, so one night after prayer meeting I waited until he was finished with the others, and then knocked on the door of his little basement office.

"I said, 'I know you're here to work with the youth group, but I wonder if you could help me with some problems.' He said, 'I'll try, but only on one condition: Do you really want God's best for your life?'

"I was really desperate. I told him I did want God's best.

"For the next half hour he asked me many questions. He had a way about him that made it easy to open up.

"Then he showed me how I was bitter toward God about the way he had made me. I realized I didn't like myself and in rejecting myself, I had rejected God's handiwork. He asked, 'How can you serve God if you aren't satisfied with the way he made you?'

"He showed me from Scripture how God had prescribed exactly how I was to look, even before I was born. He explained how God could make his strength perfect in bodily weaknesses and how he was not finished working on me yet. I realized then that God's goal was to develop inward qualities in me so that I would reflect the beauty of Christ.

"But there was an even deeper problem that Bill detected that night. And the decision he led me to make was the turning point in my life.

"For years I had struggled with the fear of being single. I was willing to serve God, but in return I was expecting him to give me a husband. I had never realized what it meant to actually abandon to God my expectation of marriage, but that night I did. It was one of the greatest struggles of my life!

"From that day I began to anticipate and even look forward to serving God as a single person. I came to value myself, as a special person whom God would use in his work."

The eyes that had been dulled by disease and debilitating trials seemed to take on new sparkle in recollection of the life-changing experience. "Without the pressure to look for a husband, I felt a new freedom. I could start setting my life in order. I made telephone calls asking for forgiveness. I dug into the Bible to find how God wanted to build my character. And I began forming close friendships, something I had never been able to do before.

"Bill Gothard said it would probably take me a year to build new thought patterns. Whenever I had a question, I would call him on the phone. I would tell him when his answers worked and when they didn't.

"When I came to Viet Nam three years ago, where do you think God put me for language study? In Danang with 10,000 GIs! I made new friends and turned down many dates. I was able to help a lot of them with personal problems because I wasn't interested in romance.

"Then in Banmethuot I was just beginning to help some of the Radê young people with their problems when I was captured. For a while I was so confident the NVAs would let us go. I just couldn't see why God didn't want me back on the job. And you know how hard I talked to some of the NVAs.

"Now I don't know what they're planning to do with us. God knows, though. We're in his hands. Hank was right in saying we should think about his greatness instead of the magnitude of our problems. I'm not going to worry about the future."

Though he wasn't the type to display much emotion, Mike was profoundly moved. The slim girl who had won his admiration for her stamina had opened her life to him.

Slowly he began to share his innermost self with her, opening long-closed doors of longings and feelings, sharing his aspirations to help the suffering Vietnamese, confiding his views of what it meant to be a Christian.

During the quiet month they spent in Buon Mega, the two came even closer. As brother and sister in Christ and partners in suffering, they found themselves able to talk about every aspect of life on the most intimate level.

Ignored by their guards, they spent long hours studying Betty's weather-beaten Bible, discussing doctrine, examining the life of Christ, considering what it meant to follow him.

"Jesus," Mike pointed out, "lived among the people and got to know their needs. So I believe I was right in living in a Radê village. Some Americans thought I was nuts. To each his own, I suppose. But I couldn't see it that way. I had to learn their customs, eat their food, share their smoky longhouses."

"You have to be close to the people," Betty agreed. "But few missionaries have been bold enough to move into their longhouses. Especially with children. We like our privacy."

"That's where the Radês are different," Mike said. "They do everything together."

"How well I know. I've gone off to a quiet spot to read my Bible and meditate, only to have a Radê come and ask sweetly, '*Amai* Betty, is something the matter?'"

"It's a hard adjustment to live as they do," Mike admitted. "But I think it's all mental. It can be done."

Hour upon hour they talked. Occasionally a guard would join in, and visiting NVAs coming to check on security would try to argue their propaganda line. But most of the time it was just Mike and Betty. Two starving prisoners with God, against a silent and implacable enemy.

CHAPTER 8

"Father, forgive..."

During the last part of August Mike and Betty heard planes flying over. Sometimes they spotted familiar markings through breaks in the clouds, but there was no way they could draw the attention of the pilots. It was so frustrating not to be seen.

They'd also heard distant artillery, evidence that the Communists had not advanced as far as they'd boasted. They knew that as the war came closer, they would be moved.

Early in September, their captors almost reversed directions and led them due north across Phuoc Long Province. As they marched through cold mountain passes and crossed deep valleys, Mike seldom lost his geographical perspective. "They're taking us deeper into their own territory," he told

Betty. "If we hold out, we may soon be in Cambodia. If we hold out. We'll just have to take it one day at a time."

They stopped first near an NVA base camp on a secluded mountaintop. It was so well camouflaged and tunneled that they didn't know they were there until halted by a patrol that suddenly appeared at the side of the trail.

A little hook-nosed NVA stepped forward. He wore the markings of the Viet Cong, but Mike immediately recognized his accent as North Vietnamese. "I am Captain Phung," he said. "I know who you are. You will be here only one night. After your meal, you will go quickly to sleep in hammocks. You must be rested for a presentation to our troops in the morning."

With nothing more to say, he turned on his heel and melted into the forest.

"What does he want?" Betty asked as they sipped their bowls of thin, tasteless rice.

"Probably just to show off two ferocious American aggressors," Mike surmised.

That was it.

Shortly after sunrise, Captain Phung popped out of the misty forest and stood fidgeting while they gulped down their breakfast—more rice. Then, conscripting a couple of guards, he ordered the Americans to follow him through the trees. A few hundred feet away they twisted between two outcroppings of rock and halted under the recess of a cliff. In the foggy air it took a few seconds to realize they were surrounded by a battalion or more of soldiers.

Captain Phung wasted no time. "I promised to show you, comrades, two American aggressors who were caught in the very act of perpetrating crimes on innocent civilians. One is a woman, but do not let that deceive you. The American imperialist profiteers even send women to fight their wars while they idle in luxury and count their dollars."

Mike and Betty stood silently, waiting for a chance to speak. None came. The officer wound up his lecture, ordered the troops back to their positions, then escorted the captives and their guards back to the main trail.

During the next two weeks they were pushed relentlessly through the rugged mountains, traveling sometimes by night and sleeping in hammocks during the day. As they pushed painfully along, they picked up dry pieces of buffalo hide to chew, a futile effort to ward off hunger pains.

At points along the way, they continued to be exhibited to North Vietnamese soldiers as trophies of success. When given half a chance, Mike tried to explain who they really were and how they were being unjustly held. Betty didn't protest any more, standing mute while their accusers spouted lies.

They were both weakening. Their hair turned gray. They lost their body hair, their nails stopped growing. Their teeth were now loose with bleeding gums; every time they bit down on anything it seemed a tooth was coming out. Once for some unexplained reason a guard gave them a tube of toothpaste which they rubbed on their gums. The taste was refreshing, but the bleeding continued.

Betty began suffering severe pains and cramps in her swollen legs. Both she and Mike were finding it hard to lift their legs. To step over a log, they had to lean down and pull up one leg at a time by hand. This difficulty finally became so acute that when stopping to rest, they had to be sure to sit against a tree. Without a tree to put their arms around and pull themselves up, they had to crawl to a supporting object.

To make their terrible plight worse, the wet foliage along the trails seemed to be alive with black, blood-sucking leeches. Mike's trousers gave him some protection, but Betty's legs were an open invitation. They attached themselves to her limbs and dug into the raw, open ulcers to satisfy their draculian appetites.

Betty had to pull and throw, pull and throw constantly to keep from being covered with the blood-thirsty creatures. They'd never been this bad before. Compared with this, the trip to the base camp before Hank died had been a lark.

Bringing up the rear, Mike saw she was losing the battle. "C'mon, Betty," he encouraged. "Don't let them get the best of you."

Pull and throw. Pull and throw. She resumed the rhythmic motion. Then he saw her arms slowing again.

"Betty, you've got to keep them off. They'll eat you alive!"

She tried again, but her movements were weak and jerky.

Mike ran ahead and begged the North Vietnamese officer who leading the march, to stop. "The leeches are killing her," he shouted.

"And your bombs are killing our people," the NVA officer declared, never breaking stride. "She'll have to keep going. The camp is another hour."

Mike got back in line behind Betty. "C'mon kid, only another hour, the NVA said. You can make it. Here, I'll help you."

Ignoring the disapproving guard behind, he began pulling leeches from Betty's legs.

When at last they reached the camp site, Betty dropped her pack and slumped to the ground. "Just let me rest a few minutes," she said flatly. "I'll get my strength back."

Mike flopped down nearby. After a few minutes, he was roused by the NVA. "Get the hammocks up," the officer ordered curtly. "Darkness will come soon."

Mike took poles cut by the Viet Cong guards and strung his and Betty's hammocks. He was stretching a strip of plastic over Betty's hammock for a roof when he saw that he needed two more poles. He looked back and saw Betty sitting up.

"Cut us a couple of little poles or vines," he said, handing her the knife entrusted to him by a guard.

"I can't do it, Mike. I don't have the strength." She began crying.

"Oh, c'mon, gal. Just a couple of little ones. Then we'll go clean up. There's a little creek over there."

Gripping the knife in a thin white hand, Betty walked a few steps into the bushes. A moment later, Mike heard her wail,

"I can't. I just can't."

Mike called her back and took the knife and tried it himself. The blade felt like a hundred pounds. He could hardly do it himself. It was clear that both he and Betty were very sick.

They had their toilets, ate the pallid rice, and then held devotions together as blackness closed in around them.

"Lord, whatever you allow is all right," Mike heard Betty say. "Forgive our enemies. They don't know what they are doing. They don't know who you are."

The next morning they were moving before sunrise. Mike noticed that Betty seemed incredibly weak and ghostly white. He carried her pack as well as his own and a bag of rice. The trail that led along the side of a mountain was narrow and crooked. Each was shadowed closely by a Viet Cong.

During the afternoon Mike and his guard fell behind, causing Mike to lose sight of Betty. This had happened before and he was not alarmed. In the early weeks of the captivity he and Hank had worried about Betty's being raped and had kept close to her. But they'd soon realized this fear was groundless. In the debilitating jungle, worn out from acute malnutrition, diseases, and fatiguing marches, men lost all sexual desire.

Then he rounded a sharp bend in the trail and saw her on the ground. The guard was bending over, pounding her with his fists, and yelling, "Get up! Get up!"

Disregarding the Viet Cong behind him, he dropped the packs and ran to her rescue. The guard beating her glared at him, saying, "She's pretending to be sick."

"Mike, I can't go on," she gasped in a tired, quaky voice. "Each time I fall, he beats me. But I can't go on."

Mike boiled with anger. He called the officer in charge and demanded that they rest.

"No. We have many kilometers yet to go today," the officer replied coldly.

"You may go on, but Miss Olsen is not going one step farther. Without proper food and medical help, she's too weak to travel. And so am I. You may drag or carry us or kill us. But we're not going."

The NVA saw that Mike was adamant and unyielding. He decided to camp.

Mike and Betty rested for a while. Then Mike asked if there was a stream close by. One of the guards pointed down the steep hill.

The two Americans started down the slope. The guards let them go alone, knowing they were too weak to walk far.

They waded into the cool water and began picking off lice, leeches, and ticks. They washed their faces, arms, and legs, all packed with ulcerous sores. Then they sat down to rest on a large flat rock.

"I'll never make it back up that steep hill, Mike. I'll have to stay here."

"You can't. They'll be down after us in a few minutes."

"You go on up and leave me here, Mike."

"No, I'm not leaving you. Come on. I'll help you."

With great difficulty, Betty struggled to her feet and caught hold of Mike's hand. With Mike pulling her they got back to the camp.

The next morning they started again. Soon they entered an area laced with narrow trails. In the thick jungle Mike and his guard became separated from Betty and her escort. When they backtracked, the guard became confused. "Look for blood," Mike advised. "She's bleeding from the leeches."

A little farther on they reached a fork and there were the telltale dark stains on the rocky ground. They followed the trail of blood and caught up.

At sundown they camped in a hollow and slept. The next morning they walked across a smooth road. "Highway 14," Mike called to Betty. "I've been through here. Duc Lap is just a little north and the Cambodian border is a few miles west."

They walked about two hours more and reached another NVA military camp. Here the officers made the usual display of Mike, but left Betty alone because she was too weak to stand.

Mike saw boxes of medicine stacked here and there with markings from Czechoslovakia and Poland. He pleaded that Betty would soon die without medical help. These NVA were as unresponsive as previous ones.

"Don't you care that a woman, a volunteer nurse who came to Vietnam to help poor lepers, will die?" he asked.

"What is that to us?" was the reply. "If she dies, that will be more rice for our brave fighting men of the revolution."

Mike returned to Betty, mumbling about the inhumanity of man.

That evening their captors enjoyed fresh roasted corn, while Betty and Mike grabbed hungrily at grains that popped out of the pan.

"Haven't you been getting enough to eat?" a visiting NVA asked.

"Rice, rice, only rice," Mike complained. "Nothing else. The corn is more nutritious."

The NVA smiled. "Very well, you may have corn," he said with a benevolent air.

He had the guards cook up a pot of corn and boil some bamboo shoots. The famished prisoners ate ravenously.

Within hours both were struck with diarrhea. "It's the bamboo shoots," Betty moaned. "They're supposed to be boiled twice. They must have boiled them only once."

Mike ground his teeth. "The lazy so-and-so's. They didn't care."

During the next two days and nights they could do nothing but stumble back and forth from their hammocks to the bushes. Then Mike's diarrhea slowed down.

But Betty's was worse. She lost all appetite, and became so weak she couldn't get out of her hammock. The dysentery was coming so fast she couldn't even raise her dress in time. She had to lie in her own defecation.

Mike pleaded with the North Vietnamese guards at least to

bring some water from the stream so he could clean her, but the request was indignantly refused. Mike did get one VC to help make a hole in Betty's hammock in hopes of relieving the situation somewhat. This proved to be of little value.

During Mike's ordeal with malaria Betty had forced him to eat. Now it was his turn.

"You have to eat, Betty. Your body's dehydrating."

"I can't, Mike. I just can't."

He begged, cajoled, argued, threatened, but she kept insisting she couldn't eat.

"Allright, if you don't eat, you'll die."

"I'm sorry. I just can't. Please, Mike. Don't try to make me. Just talk to me. Pray with me."

Mike was too weak himself to argue further. He put down the bowl of rice and began praying disconsolately. "Lord, help her. I don't know anything I can do for her. These . . . *men* . . . won't help. They don't care. I care, Lord, but what can I do? I can only turn her over to you."

"Father, forgive our captors," he heard her say. "They don't understand. I thank you that I feel no bitterness toward them. Be with my daddy and Gene. Take care of Mark and the twins. Keep Marilyn in your love. Comfort them . . ." She drifted into semiconsciousness.

Mike turned his face away. He choked on the sobs erupting deep within. He heart was breaking. He knew she was dying.

A hand pulled at his tattered collar. "Leave her," the NVA commanded. "There is nothing you can do."

Numb with shock and almost unable to stand alone, Mike had no strength to resist. They pulled him some fifty feet away and forced him into a hammock.

The next day Mike was allowed only a brief time at Betty's side. He tried to get her to eat or drink, but it was useless.

"Mike. Tell them I don't hate them. I love them. God loves them. He sent his Son to die for them.

"Mike. Dear Mike. You've been such a good friend . . .

such a good, loyal friend. My brother . . ." Again she drifted off.

The third day Betty spent in her soiled hammock was her thirty-fifth birthday. There was no celebrating. Mike begged every NVA who came around, for medicine. His entreaties were futile. The buzzing of the swarming flies was the only song to be heard.

"It's all right, Mike," she whispered reassuringly. "They can't hurt me any more. . . The Lord is my Shepherd, I shall not want . . . His strength is made perfect in my weakness . . . neither death, nor life, nor angels, nor principalities, nor powers, nor things present, nor things to come, nor height, nor depth, shall be able to separate us from the love of God, which is in Christ Jesus our Lord." Her voice trailed off in a thin whisper.

By the fourth day Mike was ready to crack. "Why don't you help her?" he groaned to the guards. "How can you let her die like this? An innocent woman who loves the Vietnamese people. A nurse who has saved many lives."

The captors acted as if he didn't exist. He didn't have enough strength to lash out at them. Mercifully, Betty was so weak by this time that she was only vaguely aware of her circumstances.

Mike awoke from a nightmarish sleep the fifth day. He struggled out of the hammock and walked uneasily to Betty's hammock. Her slim form lay in quiet repose. He called her name softly. No answer.

His hand groped for her pulse. He waited. He called again. No answer.

He turned away, numbed, shaking his head in grief and despair.

He was alone.

CHAPTER 9

March of Death

At last the NVAs gave Betty some attention. An army doctor examined her, pronounced her dead, and ordered immediate burial.

Mike heard the guards digging in a grove of bamboo. Sometime later—he was too weak and shaken to keep track of the time—they pulled her body from the hammock and carried it to the grave like a sack of potatoes. There was no ceremony, no service, just thud and then the scratchy shoveling of loose dirt.

Dazed and bewildered, Mike could not speak. The most unselfish person he had ever known was dead. Never again in this life would he hear her infectious laugh, see her encouraging smile, feel her soft hand on his feverish head. He knew he'd lived this long only because of the girl he had once thought to be a stick-in-the-mud.

Now he was alone, with only recollections of Betty and Hank—and his faith in their God. "Lord, I can't make it without you," he prayed. "I have no one else."

His captors didn't keep him long at the scene of Betty's death. He was glad, for he was ready to leave this place of pain. The last five days had been the greatest agony of his life. The sight of Betty lying in the dirty hammock; the sound of her voice begging for help; then when help was refused, her asking God's forgiveness for those who would let her die: these memories would be etched in his mind forever.

He stumbled along behind a guard as the sun rose behind them. The NVA officer up ahead did not announce, "We are now entering Cambodia." There were no border markers. But having crossed Highway 14 with Betty, Mike knew they were in the fabled land of the Khmers who had once dominated much of southeast Asia.

"Neutral" Cambodia—sanctuary of the North Vietnamese. Mike knew no search party would come here. The NVAs could hold him as long as they wished, deny that he ever existed, or have their Viet Cong spokesmen say he'd died of disease in the South Vietnamese jungle. With captors who seemed not to care whether he lived or died, the future looked abysmally bleak.

Suddenly he heard the rumble and roar of trucks. Breaking out of the forest, he was showered with dust. As far as he could see in either direction, a steady line of trucks was moving along a branch of the Ho Chi Minh Trail. The trucks were loaded with troops, supplies, and ammunitions going south. Others rattled along empty, going north. Throughout Mike's five years in Viet Nam, the North Vietnamese had maintained that they had no troops in either South Vietnam or "neutral" Cambodia. Here is proof of the big lie, he thought bitterly.

They turned north, marching along the dusty highway shaded by trees, left purposely to camouflage the road from planes. Kilometer after kilometer Mike walked, ten to twelve hours a day, bare feet pounding the rocky shoulders, shin bones feeling as if they were being broken into splinters. The never-ending traffic rolled past.

When his left knee began aching painfully, they wouldn't stop. "Push on, push on," the NVA in charge demanded. He could only pray, grit his teeth, and keep limping, throwing all the weight he could on his right foot.

After several days they turned off on a side road into a more secluded area and passed armed sentries. Squinting ahead through the trees Mike made out a compound of small thatched-roof buildings.

Then he heard voices speaking English. Smooth and without accent. Was he dreaming? No, they were calling, asking his name and outfit. He answered in a slow, croaky voice, his throat tight with excitement. Except for Betty and Hank, these were the first Americans he'd seen in almost a year.

Mike was so thrilled to see friendly people, people from home, that he felt like dancing a jig despite the sore knee. There were 14 GIs of different rank, captured in various parts of South Vietnam. They all shook his hand and patted him on the back. "Welcome to Camp 102," a smiling black sergeant said.

The prisoners slept under tight guard, but during the day they were permitted to fraternize. Mike was eager to hear their stories and tell his.

His voice shook when he told how Betty had died. "They had medicines close by. They said she was of no political value, and let her die. Of no value? She was the bravest, kindest, and sweetest person I ever knew."

Though toughened by the brutality of war, the POWs listened with moist eyes as Mike told of his experiences with the two missionaries. When he described how Betty kept him from dying during the nightmarish thirty-five days of malaria, his voice trembled again. "Without her, I wouldn't be here," he whispered huskily. "If only I could have saved her life. God knows, I tried.

"When I went into the jungle with those missionaries," he added, "I wasn't on close terms with the Almighty. Betty and Hank helped me find real faith. This is all that's kept me alive."

Mike's testimony raised the morale of the camp. While they weren't permitted to hold religious services as a group, each could pray individually. Their prayers and support of each other kept them strong in faith.

Whenever the prisoners mentioned the Geneva Convention agreement on treatment of POWs, the NVAs laughed in their faces. The Geneva agreement required that POWs be treated humanely, given proper food and shelter, and be permitted to receive mail and parcels from home. Prisoners were not to be tortured or forced to write confessions. "War criminals have no rights" was the stock answer,

The diet of rice and occasional monkey meat was barely enough to keep them alive. Sergeant Gale Kearns, who'd been wounded in the right arm, suffered the most. Because he was so weak and suffering from malnutrition, his fellow prisoners feared he might die unless he got more to eat.

They asked one of the NVA officers to increase his allotment. "No, he is a war criminal and does not deserve special treatment," the officer replied coldly.

"You aren't honoring the Geneva agreement," Mike declared flatly. "You're treating us worse than animals."

The officer stared glassily at Mike, who refused to blink.

"If you are humane and just as you claim," Mike said, "you will give this man more food."

"He is a war criminal. You are all war criminals. You have no rights," the NVA insisted.

"Then let us give him some of our food."

The NVA was not touched. He refused to permit even this act of mercy.

Another officer, whom they called "Charger," taunted them with news that Dr. Martin Luther King and Senator Robert Kennedy had been assassinated. "Your country is controlled by criminals," he declared pompously. "But now that Dr. King is dead, the blacks will rise up."

Charger singled out the one black in the camp for special attention. "Both your people and mine are oppressed by the American white capitalists," the NVA told Sergeant McMurray. "Why not side with the brave Vietnamese people against the American policies of war and genocide?"

"Just what is it you want me to do?" the black Detroiter asked.

Charger put a tape recorder on the table and handed Sergeant McMurray the microphone. "Tell your fellow black soldiers that America is a racist nation. Ask them to lay down their arms and stop fighting against their Vietnamese brothers. We will broadcast your message to them."

The NVA turned on the tape recorder and waited expectantly. To his embarrassment, the black soldier declared, "I believe in my country. I will always be loyal. I will not speak against America."

"You are acting very foolishly," Charger replied. "But I will give you another chance to help your people and mine."

The black American glared back defiantly. "No! Never!"

At infrequent intervals the camp loudspeaker was turned up for the prisoners to listen to Radio Hanoi. Every show was so much alike that eventually they could predict what the speaker would say next. Over and over, they heard the slogans:

"America is run by capitalist, war-mongering profiteers from Wall Street.

"These warmongers have deceived the people about the illegal, unjust, and immoral war.

"The Vietnamese people want only freedom, happiness, and independence.

"American soldiers are being used as cannon fodder for the Wall Street capitalists."

The news from America, as Radio Hanoi reported it, was so obviously distorted that they didn't know what was true and what wasn't. One broadcast presented a lecture by a doctor on the effects of malnutrition. The NVA assumption was that millions of Americans were like this.

Mike was scrubbing his skinny naked frame when this program began blaring from the loudspeakers. Having nothing better to do, he presented his own parody of the descriptions.

"The teeth become loose . . ." the speaker said.

Mike wiggled his mouth. "Yes."

"The stomach is distended and bloated . . ." Mike pushed out his inflated stomach. "Yes."

"The collarbones protrude . . ." Mike raised his bony shoulders up and down. "Yes."

Mike continued mimicking every symptom until the announcer concluded: "This is the condition of millions of starving Americans." Then he shouted loud enough for everyone in the camp to hear, "Yes, and there are fifteen more right here!"

Fall drooped into winter while the prisoners kept count of every boring, listless day. When the first anniversary of Mike's capture came, it seemed to him he'd been gone a lifetime.

The prisoners treasured every pin, piece of paper, and scrap of metal they could find. Mike made playing cards from tissue paper and whittled a chess set from bamboo. He could only rummage in his memory for verses of Scripture and Bible stories from his time with Betty and Hank. The NVAs had confiscated Betty's lumpy, worn Bible after her death. Her comb was the only possession he had been able to keep. He hoped to give it to her sister Marilyn someday.

The food got no better. Their rations of rice were cut.

Whenever one of the Americans protested, he was told by an NVA, "You will suffice"—whatever that meant. Mike heard this answer so often that he wrote a mournful song:

> *In Camp one oh two,*
> *Somewhere north of Pleiku*
> *The Dink he served bugs,*
> *The Dink he served stones.*
> *We never got meat,*
> *Not even the bones.*
> *We went to the Dink;*
> *We asked for some rice;*
> *All that he told us was*
> *You will suffice—*
> *You will suffice.*

Spring turned to summer and there was no hint of when they might be leaving. The fifteen prisoners saw no other Americans, but NVA groups dropped by periodically. For any arriving NVA willing to talk, Mike had a standard question: "Have you seen an American lady doctor and two civilian men in one of your camps?" Every answer was negative. In view of what had happened to Hank Blood and Betty Olsen, Mike could understand how the missionaries captured in 1962 could have vanished in the jungle.

In late July 1969 they heard indirectly of a major news event. The Hanoi propagandist was saying that America was capable of putting a man on the moon but couldn't end the Viet Nam War. A few days later they heard a broadcast praising the great scientific technology of the Socialist world that had landed a robot machine on the moon.

But the American achievement was of little comfort to the fifteen prisoners. They couldn't eat moon landings. They could only live from one day to the next, hoping and praying for a miracle.

One of the thinnest POWs was Billy Smith, a boyish, fresh-faced young private from Boston. He was one of Mike's favorites. Hour after hour they sat recalling memories of home and discussing what they would do when they were released.

When they were finally marched out of the camp in September 1969, Mike hung close to Billy, concerned that he might fall. This was, as they later learned, near the time of Ho Chi Minh's death—a time when prisoners in North Viet Nam began getting better treatment. But there was no letup in the rigors of the men from Camp 102.

As they stumbled northward, with Mike limping from his old knee injury, trucks roared past without slowing. Mike begged the guards to stop one of the trucks and give Billy a ride. They laughed and kept going.

Finally what Mike had feared happened. Billy collapsed on the road. He and some other prisoners started to the private's aid, but were restrained.

While the Americans watched in horror, the NVAs kicked the boy into the bushes, where one picked up a rock and smashed his head. Billy was beyond help now.

The Americans were ordered on. Hour after dusty hour they trudged up the Trail, each day fearing they could not last another. Quite often they heard dull booms in the west, evidence that American planes were keeping the North Vietnamese under heavy pressure.

Just when Mike felt he could go no farther, they stopped at a military camp. The next morning he was unable to walk. His left knee was too sore to stand on. On the right, he had lost all feeling in his side, arm, and leg.

A guard saw him trying to get up and called the camp doctor. The NVA medic gave him the first medical attention he'd received since being captured: a semisterile intravenous infusion of sugar and water. When after an hour only about an inch had drained from the pint bottle, the doctor poured what was left into a dirty bowl and ordered Mike to drink it.

Mercilessly, the soldiers forced the fifteen prisoners to resume the torturous trek. How he kept going, Mike himself didn't know. He could only cry inwardly to God for strength and keep moving his pain-wracked body.

From the distance they had traveled since leaving Camp 102. Mike knew they were in Laos now. Did they plan to force them to walk all the way to Hanoi?

He was dimly aware of crossing Highway 9, which runs east-west across South Viet Nam, just below the Demilitarized Zone, and into Laos. Just beyond the highway the guards led them down a side road. A short distance on they reached a field hospital.

"You will rest here and receive medical treatment," an NVA doctor told them.

Dizzy and feverish, Mike squinted through his glasses that were held together with a makeshift piece of rubber. He'd broken them several days before. His fellow prisoners looked like pictures of Jews in a Nazi prison camp. Disheveled and dirty, with hair turned white from insufficient diet, and tottering on swollen legs, they were one step from the grave.

He didn't need a mirror to realize he was seeing himself.

CHAPTER 10

Moment of Destiny

At the hospital an NVA doctor briskly examined Mike and diagnosed his condition as advanced beriberi and severe scurvy, both caused by extreme malnutrition. Mike could have told him that himself, for at Oregon State University he had taken courses in human nutrition.

The medic immediately ordered repeated intravenous injections of Vitamins B and C, plus more vitamins to be given subcutaneously. Because Mike was so emaciated, they tried—unsuccessfully—to feed him with injections of glucose. When it was evident this wasn't working, they let him drink the solutions.

After three weeks in the NVA field hospital, Mike was not a new man. But the fever was gone and the vitamin deficiency was less severe. At least he could walk. The health of the other prisoners had improved also, but Sergeant Kearns's injured arm hung limp by his side. It had been neglected too long.

Forced to resume the march in October, they turned east into North Viet Nam just above the 38th parallel. Days and days they walked, driven by shouting and goading guards. Each day seemed worse than the one before. Mike ached all over. Breathing was difficult. His heart pounded under a skeleton cage of ribs. With the sole of his right foot gone and gravel pinching tender flesh, every step was torture. But he wouldn't complain. His buddies were hurting, too.

How long, O Lord, how long? How much more could they stand?

Drawing on strength beyond themselves, they kept stumbling ahead, gasping mutual encouragement, trying to get through one day at a time, all remembering the fate of Private Billy Smith.

Then when it seemed the prisoners could go no farther, the guards stopped a truck and shoved them in. They were driven to a small prison south of Hanoi and given faded uniforms.

When Mike had eaten and rested, the political commissar summoned him for an interview.

Patting a thick folder, the NVA said smugly, "We have a large file on you, Mr. Benge. We know all about your CIA activities for your American Department of State. It will be to your benefit to confess."

Because of his broken glasses, Mike had to tilt his head to look at the officer. "Confess what?" he demanded.

"That you are a spy."

Mike pulled back his bony shoulders and frowned. Not expecting to be believed, he again described his work and why he had come to Viet Nam. Then he quoted the Geneva Agreement on treatment of prisoners.

The NVA merely laughed. "We will give you some time to think. Perhaps then you will be more truthful."

A guard grasped Mike's arm, led him down a corridor, and

shoved him into a dark room. It took a while for his eyes to adjust. The room was about nine by ten. The walls were painted black. The only ventilation and light came from a small round hole near the eight-foot ceiling and another hole under the door.

He felt something furry rub against his bare foot. Peering down, he counted seven rats. When he kicked at the rodents, they merely ran to the other side of the room. In a couple of hours or so a guard opened the door and shoved in a bowl of cabbage soup. He ate. Slept. The guard brought another bowl of soup plus a small loaf of brown French bread. He ate again. Shooed rats. Slapped at flies. Did exercises, physical and mental. Prayed for strength.

He heard a tap, then a scratch. Tap-tap-scratch. Someone was trying to communicate in Morse Code. Mike answered back with his name. The man at the other end gave his.

Mike was tied into the prison network. By coughing, whistling, scratching, and tapping they shared stories, swapped jokes, mocked their captors, and kept everyone informed about the latest interrogations. When a new prisoner was brought in, everyone knew within hours his name, outfit, and circumstances of capture. When a code was broken and violators punished, the prisoners changed to another.

All took turns in facing the camp commander. Mike was among the most adamant in refusing to make false confessions and write antiwar statements. He was always demanding that the North Vietnamese start observing the Geneva Agreement. For such obstinacy, he was beaten with a rubber hose and forced to sit at attention for up to sixteen hours a day. He was also required to bow at a 90 degree angle whenever the guard peeped through his door.

The days dragged by until one morning an NVA poked his head in and said, "Mr. Benge, do you know what holiday is coming?"

Mike thought and thought. He finally had to admit, "I don't know."

"Ah, Mr. Benge, you do not know American traditions and

holidays very well. On this holiday you are not permitted to eat meat." Mike chuckled bitterly. He had had no meat in months.

A couple of days later the guard brought around a soybean cake—"for a special treat," he said. Then he turned on a radio and invited Mike to listen to an Easter service broadcast from Hanoi.

A tremulous Vietnamese voice announced in English: "'Render unto God that which is God's and render unto Ceasar that which is Caesar's.' Why do you not allow the Vietnamese people to have their freedom? Why do you continue your evil war of aggression?" The propaganda was so blatant, so obvious. How stupid do they think we are? Mike thought.

A few days after Easter Mike was called again before the political commissar. The NVA repeated the old demands: confess and write a statement of repentance. Mike refused and again called for adherence to the rules of the Geneva Agreement.

The commissar's face reddened with anger. "You are our prisoner. We will do with you as we wish." He called the guard and ordered that Mike be beaten and put back in his cell.

Spring passed into the hot months of summer. Mike sat in his black cell, praying, waiting, hoping, kicking rats, slapping flies. He relived old memories, devised new plans for helping the Vietnamese tribal people, recited to himself the Bible verses and stories he had learned from Betty and Hank.

Then in his eleventh month of solitary (November 1970), he heard Hanoi Radio admit that U.S. commandos had tried —unsuccessfully,—to rescue some prisoners. Soon after that, the NVAs loaded Mike and his companions in the country camp into trucks and moved them to a more secure prison near Hanoi.

Mike's hopes for roommates were dashed when he was put back in solitary. Six days passed. The prospect of more interminable isolation lay heavy on his mind. He considered giving in and writing a letter. He could say what the NVAs wanted him to say in a way that would indicate to American readers he was writing lies. At least his mother, stepfather, and sister would know he was alive.

He was almost ready to write, when on the seventh day they moved him without explanation to a room with two roommates. He felt that with their encouragement he could hold out.

Through communications the three learned there were 102 Americans in the old warehouse that had been converted to a prison. It was called Plantation Gardens, but Mike suggested changing the name to the Animal Farm because some prisoners got more lenient treatment than others. He dubbed one section the Bull Pen, another the Sheep Shed, and the area he and his roommates were in, the Hog House.

The NVAs knew that the prisoners were talking to one another, and set out to find and break a weak link. The POWs knew someone was finking when their captors started beating certain resistance leaders, including Mike.

Mike himself finally discovered the leak and changed the code and the room numbers. Again the NVAs were baffled.

As in the last prison, Mike passed on the accounts of how Betty and Hank had died, and shared his own personal experience with God. Many of his fellow prisoners testified of finding a closeness to God they'd never known before.

Sergeant Joe Anzaldua, a twenty-two-year-old Marine of Spanish descent, from Corpus Christi, Texas, told of being captured in South Viet Nam and taken to join twelve other Americans who were the survivors of a contingent of twenty-five prisoners. The thirteen missing, two of whom were German nurses working at a civilian hospital, had died of malnutrition and dysentery. "When I came into the camp," Sergeant Anzaldua recalled, "a black man named Isaiah McMillan was reading Scripture to a boy named Dennis Hammon. Dennis was near death, but before dying he found his Creator and came to love God's Word. Before long, I was talking to my Lord in the most personal way possible."

Mike and Joe Anzaldua found they had a lot in common. Both spoke Vietnamese. Both had subsisted on rice, manioc, and roasted lizards and bugs. Both had been close to death.

"I came down with meningitis," Joe said. "I thought every day was going to be my last. I had a pretty strong faith, but I kept asking God, 'Why?' A couple of guards asked me, 'If your God is so good, why can't he get you out of here?' I tried to explain that he didn't work that way, but they were never convinced."

The Animal Farm POWs were forbidden to participate in religious services or exercises, except during holidays. For Christmas 1970, Mike was allowed to paint six biblical pictures for aids in worship. Although he had studied drawing only in high school, he set to work, sketching the Nativity and other scenes from the life of Jesus. The NVAs allowed him to hang these alongside a cross in a "Christmas room." Then on Christmas morning, a little guard they called "Cheese" came and said, "You are now permitted to go one at a time and pray to your God."

A few days after Christmas, Mike was summoned before the political commissar. "You will please to write about the pacification program among the civilians in South Viet Nam," the NVA said.

"And if I don't?" Mike asked.

"You will be given special education."

Mike was sure he meant beatings followed by propaganda and another stretch in isolation. Reluctantly, he took the pencil and paper and wrote about an imaginary goof-up without mentioning any names or nationalities.

"You left out the part about the Americans," the commissar said after reading the paper.

Mike forced a grin. "Yes. This is a new style of writing started in America by a man named Alfred Hitchcock."

The commissar appeared puzzled. Then he said, "You will please to write about American failures in pacification."

Mike started again and wrote page after page of redundant nothingness. The commissar was not amused. "When are you going to cooperate?"

"When are you going to observe the Geneva Agreement?" Mike shot back.

The NVA eyed him coldly. "You are belligerent, obstinate, and odious."

"Yes, sir," Mike responded. "I am odious because I am so seldom allowed to take a bath."

"Silence! You are acting like a commander. This is a crime punishable by death. Don't you realize we can kill you at any time?"

He paused, waiting for Mike to speak.

"Aren't you afraid?"

Mike adjusted his glasses and looked hard at the NVA. "I am very sorry, but you do not have the power of life or death over me. I should already have died twice. The only reason I did not is that Somebody up there is looking after me. He has the power of life or death over me. You do not have that power. If God chooses that I die today, I will die. You cannot kill me."

The commissar sat silent, glaring at Mike as if he were crazy. Finally he shouted, "Enough! Guard, take him back to his room."

Mike sat in his room waiting for something to happen. He was still waiting when Cheese came to take him and his two roommates out for exercise.

In the exercise yard Mike picked up a stick of bamboo, a string, and a piece of wire. He carried these back to his room and used a stolen razor blade to whittle out a cross. Then he hung the cross defiantly around his neck.

The next session with the commissar didn't end so well. After turning in the usual written nonsense, Mike asked for a clean water bucket to wash in before meals. "The defecation bucket we are required to use doesn't smell so good," he explained.

The NVA's response was to summon guards for a beating.

They pounded him unmercifully with clubs, but because Mike knew judo, he was able to protect his groin, kidneys, bowels, the back of his head, and other especially vulnerable parts of his body.

When the beating was done, they tied his hands behind his back and attached leg irons. Then the commissar and another officer began kicking him in the head and ears and mouth, demanding, "Will you confess?"

When Mike groaned, "Yes," they stopped. "I confess," he gasped, "that I failed to wash my face in the defecation bucket."

Mike continued to be "belligerent, obstinate, and odious" in the eyes of his captors. He was repeatedly beaten and sometimes kept for weeks at a time in isolation. Many of his fellow prisoners suffered similar treatment.

However, they were never denied specially selected reading material. They got a steady diet of the Communist *Daily Worker* and *The Great Speckled Bird*, an antiwar, sex tabloid published in the United States. When passing out the *Bird*, the NVAs would call attention to articles lauding homosexuality and sexual promiscuity, pointing to these as evidence of social decadence in the U.S. In contrast they were always praising Communism as the solution to all evils. "We will build a perfect state in which machines will one day do all labor," they predicted. "There will be no wars. Everybody will live together in peace. In such a society, God will be only a hindrance."

In September 1971 Mike and some other Animal Farm prisoners were transferred to another prison, Mike's third in North Viet Nam. With elections coming up in both North and South Viet Nam and in the U.S., the NVAs made politics a key topic of discussion.

When they cited the two-man election in South Viet Nam as evidence of a corrupt dictatorship, Mike asked the commissar, "How can you say this when you have only one man running for each office in your country?"

"Oh, we are united. Everybody agrees with the government—except a few reactionaries," he conceded.

Mike tried to explain how democracy operated in the United States. "Political candidates can run against the government. They can criticize the government, point out its faults. When election comes, voters have a choice from the smallest to the highest office."

The NVAs didn't seem to understand how this could possibly be.

The following January, Mike was moved with a group of prisoners to the celebrated Hanoi Hilton in downtown Hanoi. Some of the over 500 POWs in "Hilton" were quartered in groups of fifteen, thirty, and more in assembly rooms. Mike, however, was put in a whitewashed room about ten by ten with four roommates.

It was equipped with bunk beds built onto the walls, with each bed having built-in leg stocks at the foot. All the guards had to do to keep a man in bed was to place his ankles in the iron bracelets and snap them shut.

A large window high on one wall was covered by a double set of bars. Through the window Mike could see a high wall ridged by jagged slivers of embedded glass.

Communication took a little more ingenuity here, for cell walls were not joined. A hall or some other air space lay between each room and the next, making tapping noises difficult to hear. Still they found ways to talk from room to room and soon Mike was "broadcasting" the story of how his missionary companions had died on the trail.

His first nine months in the "Hilton" were the hardest. As in previous camps, the NVAs wanted statements and confessions for use in propaganda. Mike was as uncooperative as before, writing pages of foolishness that kept his roommates in stitches. And as before he kept reminding the NVA officers that they weren't complying with the Geneva Agreement for treatment of prisoners.

Here, too, he was called "belligerent, obstinate, and

odious," and rewarded with more beatings. He was forced to kneel with hands up for painfully long periods of time. He was placed in solitary confinement. Through the network he learned of men who had withstood worse abuse and torture for over seven years.

Mike and his roommates were not allowed to participate in the group religious services permitted men in other sections of the Hilton. They could only pray in their rooms and whisper assurances from hymns and Bible verses.

In conversations about religion, various NVA officers had always assured Mike there was freedom of religion in North Viet Nam. When a Hilton NVA made this statement, Mike asked for a New Testament.

"We don't have one in English," he was told.

"Then French will do."

"Sorry, we have Bibles only in Latin," the officer rejoined.

"Bring us that," Mike asked. But it never arrived.

Later a new prisoner brought in a New Testament taken from the body of a dead GI. The precious book was passed from prisoner to prisoner. Mike had it for two wonderful days.

In October 1972 the prisoners were told that peace negotiations were in process. They were put on a heavy starch diet to fatten them up. When the negotiations stalled, their rations were cut again.

The food improved just before Christmas when they heard over the loudspeakers that U.S. B-52 raids had been launched against Hanoi. Mike and his roommates stood under their window and saw the bombs falling. One missile fell close enough to kill a bird within sight.

In January the Hilton underwent an amazing transformation. Instruments of torture were removed. The courtyard was cleaned. A volleyball net was strung across the court. Basketball backboards were nailed into place.

The jubilant prisoners began expecting to be released any day.

An officer came to Mike's room with pen and paper. "Since the hostilities are ending, we will allow you the privilege to write a letter home."

"I've waited almost five years without sending or receiving a letter from home," Mike said. "I can wait a little longer."

The NVA left and returned later. Again Mike refused. But the third time he agreed to write and when the letter was finished he handed it to the officer.

The officer read it and objected to Mike telling his folks, "Contact Sister Benedict at her convent in Saigon and tell her I am all right."

"We cannot permit you to use the word *convent*."

"There is nothing in the peace agreements that says I cannot write that," Mike declared.

"We tell you you cannot."

"Show it to me in the agreement," Mike demanded.

"We say you can't," the NVA snapped in impatience.

"Then take your paper and cram it," Mike said in disgust and threw the letter in his face.

In February communications reported the arrival of two male missionary prisoners from Laos. But they were not Archie Mitchell and Dan Gerber, who had been captured in 1962 and about whom Mike had asked so many times. Samuel Mattix and Alexander Wirt had been marched forty days up the Ho Chi Minh Trail from Laos to Hanoi. GI prisoners coming from Laos reported more chilling news. They told of two women missionaries being bound by Communist soldiers and left to burn to death in their flaming hut.[*]

Mike was still reflecting on this atrocity when about a hundred men were called out and fitted with new clothes. To his consternation, he wasn't among them. He wondered why, for a story had swept the prison that civilians were to go first.

---

[*]Evelyn Anderson of Coldwater, Michigan, and Beatrice Kosin of Federal Way, Washington, members of the Christian Missions in Many Lands, a Brethren-affiliated mission.

The next day, February 12, this first contingent of to-be-released POWs left the prison in buses.

A second group followed and still Mike waited, hoping every day he would be next.

February ended and still his name hadn't been called. Why were the NVAs waiting so long?

Finally: "Mr. Benge. You are pleased to follow me."

Had the time really come?

Mike followed the NVA out the door and down the corridor to an area where other prisoners were changing into new uniforms.

His heart beat wildly. He was so excited he could hardly get his feet into the trouser legs.

The guards were standing around looking solemn. Mike suddenly felt sorry for them. All they knew was the propaganda that was dinned into their ears day after day.

An NVA officer stepped out to lead the prisoners to the bus. A few minutes later they were at Gia Lam Airport walking toward the most beautiful plane Mike had ever seen. He wanted to kiss every square inch of the big C-141 Starlifter with the Red Crosses on its tail, to hug the escort officer who shook his hand at the foot of the stairs.

He climbed into the plane and found a seat with the other prisoners. Besides Mike, there were two more American civilians, two German medical workers, two Filipino employees of the Voice of America, and twenty-seven GIs on board.

The big plane taxied across to the main runway. The seconds seemed to Mike like hours as the plane stopped, then swung into position for takeoff. Then his heart rushed into his throat as the motors roared.

It sped down the runway. Clickety, click, click over the cracks in the pavement. Faster and faster. Mike held his breath, waiting... Was it all a cruel dream?

The wheels lifted off the ground. A tremendous shout drowned out the roar of the engines.

"God bless America, land that I love..." someone

croaked, too full of emotion to sing clearly.

"Stand beside her and guide her . . ." Mike joined in with the others.

Two hours later they landed at Clark Field in the Philippines. The cheering crowd, the waving flags, the bobbing signs brought more tears of gratitude to Mike's eyes.

Since there were two Filipinos in their group, President Ferdinand E. Marcos headed up the welcoming committee. With thoughts whirling, Mike solemnly shook the Filipino's hand. As he was greeted by the American Ambassador and a line of U.S. military brass a feeling of unreality gripped him.

"It's real," he kept reminding himself. "I'm free! I'm really free! I'm on my way home!"

A short religious service was held at the Clark Field's military hospital. Then the returnees trooped to telephones to place calls to loved ones in the States.

As Mike waited for the connection to be completed he wondered if he would even remember what she sounded like. It had been so long.

"Hello," said an anxious woman. Emotion overwhelmed Mike as he immediately recognized the beloved voice.

"Hello?" she repeated, as Mike tried to control himself enough to speak.

"Mother," he blurted. "It's Mike."

"Oh, Mike! Darling. It's really you! We've waited so long. All these years. We didn't even know you were alive. There'd been no reports about you until the names were released of the prisoners who had been set free.

"How are you, Son? I can't wait to see you."

Still rejoicing over the phone calls, the former prisoners entered the dining hall. Mike felt he was in a dream as mounds of food were placed before him. Thick, juicy steaks, heaps of mashed potatoes, steaming fried eggs, and gallons of delicious ice cream. He ate until he hurt. Then ate some more.

After a quick medical check Mike was told he had a visitor. As he entered the reception room he recognized the tall woman—it was Vange Blood, waiting stoically to ask her question.

"Is it true, Mike? Is Hank really dead? I've heard so many conflicting reports over the last years, I can hardly believe this one is real."

"Yes, Vange," Mike replied tenderly. "He's dead. I helped bury him."

A long moment passed.

"Well," she responded slowly, fighting to control the tears that streamed down her cheeks. "At least I know for sure. The uncertainty has been hard to bear. Tell me about it."

Haltingly, Mike recalled Hank's trials on the trail. His witness. And his death. "His last thoughts were of you and the children," he told her. "And he hoped you would continue working on the Mnong translation."

"I knew he would," Vange replied, managing a weak smile. "That's why the children and I are here at Wycliffe's Philippine base. It's slow, hard work, but I'll finish it," she declared with quiet determination.

Mike nodded his approval, then asked, "What happened after we left Banmethuot? Carolyn Griswold—Betty was so concerned about her. Did she make it? And Marie—Marie Ziemer. She was wounded too. Did they survive?"

"The tribespeople helped get Marie, Carolyn, my children and me to the U.S. military advisers' headquarters. We were evacuated from there to the U.S. Army's 8th Field Hospital at Nha Trang.

"Carolyn never regained consciousness. She died at Nha Trang. Marie had an injured ear drum and severe shrapnel wounds along her left side and leg. She had it pretty rough for a while, but she's doing fine now. Little Cathy and I suffered only minor cuts."

"And your Cindy?" Mike asked. "Hank was so concerned because she was separated from her family during the crisis."

"We were reunited with Cindy at Nha Trang. She had had a narrow escape at Kontum, but she had been protected by the missionaries there. Dalat, Pleiku, Hue and some other places were hit hard too. But the only missionary casualties were at Banmethuot.

"The bodies of Bob Ziemer, Mr. Griswold and Carolyn were flown home for burial. Ruth Wilting and Ed and Marie Thompson were left in the garbage pit where they died. A beautiful memorial has been erected around the grave."

"And Pastor Ngue, the Radê preacher? Was his escape successful? Did he make it back?"

"Yes, he did," Vange replied. "But I was told that he looked so pitiful that his wife had difficulty recognizing him. He had quite a story to tell of escaping from a tiger, swimming deep rivers, even falling into a snake pit.

"He tried to get the U.S. Special Forces to send out a rescue team. But they wouldn't follow his plan."

"When I get back to Viet Nam, I'll sure look him up," Mike vowed. "He's quite a man."

"When you get back!" Vange exclaimed. "You mean after all you've been through you're planning on returning?"

"Certainly. Those tribespeople are going to need all the help they can get," Mike declared as he wearily rose on tottering legs. "It's nearly time for the flight to the mainland," he explained.

"Did you receive a letter from Hank after he was captured?" he asked as they walked along.

"A letter?" Vange asked, perplexed. "What letter?"

"That so-and-so!" Mike scowled in disgust. "He told us he had given you the letter personally. Typical!"

As the two were about to separate, Mike had one more question. "Hank's tribal convert, Tang? How's he doing?" Mike asked hesitantly.

Vange smiled. "Tang is a beautiful Christian, Mike. After Hank was captured he grew in the Lord by leaps and bounds and has become the spiritual leader of his people. He's won thousands of tribal people to Christ."

Mike swallowed hard, trying to control his emotions. "Then Hank's sacrifice wasn't in vain," he declared.

"No, I know it wasn't," Vange agreed. "A real revival has

broken out among the tribespeople. The buildings that were destroyed have been rebuilt. The work goes on."

Arriving in the U.S., Mike had a brief but joyous reunion with his family. "Just wait until you get home from your medical treatment," his mother told him. "All of Morrow County is planning a hero's welcome for you like it's never had before."

After being examined by the doctors at the Naval Medical Center in suburban Washington, D.C., Mike was told, "You are in surprisingly good condition, considering the severe malnutrition and other prison abuses you've endured. With extra vitamins, minerals, iodine, and a high protein diet you'll soon be almost as good as new.

"There had been some damage to your eyes, but in time we feel your full visual powers will be restored. As a matter of fact, you're in such good condition we've agreed to make a special exception and allow you to have some visitors. There are some mission leaders who would like a firsthand report of what happened to their missionaries."

"Of course," Mike replied. "There must be many people who have prayed for Hank and Betty over the years who want to know. I'll share with them as well as I can."

The Wycliffe and Alliance leaders filed in. Mike greeted them. Then in slow, hesitant speech, he described the experiences in captivity, and how the missionaries had died.

"I can't express to you how very much Betty and Hank meant to me," he declared. "I grew up in a good Christian home, but I never made a full commitment of my life to God until I turned to him in the jungle.

"I'll never forget those two wonderful friends. Both praying and talking to me about what it means to be a Christian. Betty saving my life when I was blind and delirious from malaria. Then . . ."

His listeners waited patiently as he struggled to regain his composure.

"I . . . I find it hard to talk about Betty . . . what they did to her . . . how they let her die in that hammock." Mike covered his face with thin hands.

The visitors waited in sympathetic silence.

"I wanted to help her . . . I tried. They wouldn't let me. . . And she was always asking God to forgive them. . . She never hated or was bitter . . . To the end she loved everyone."

After a few moments one of the Alliance men quietly said, "Mike, did you learn anything about our missionaries captured in 1962? Dr. Ardel Vietti, Archie Mitchell, and the Mennonite, Dan Gerber. We've investigated every possible channel to find if they are still alive, and if they are, to get them back."

Mike slowly shook his head. "Everywhere I went, I asked about them. No one knew anything, or if they did they wouldn't tell me."

Mike talked on for over an hour while the visitors took notes. Before they left they bowed for a prayer of thanksgiving and praise. As they were reaching for their coats, Mike added one more thought.

"There's a lesson to learn from all this," he declared. "The Communists tried to wipe out Christianity in the Banmethuot area. But they failed, didn't they?"

Afterword

On March 20, 1973, Mike Benge was given the U.S. Department of State *Award for Heroism* "for personally insuring the safety of eleven American civilians during the *Tet* offensive of 1968."

On May 23, 1973, Mike was presented the Department of State's *Award for Valor* "for exceptional courage and stamina while held as a prisoner of war in Viet Nam." The citation to Mike and five other American civilian POWs further stated:

> *Each of them demonstrated exceptional valor in helping care for fellow prisoners, in resisting efforts of their captors to break their spirits, and in preserving their own mental and physical strength. Their very survival under the grim conditions of their captivity—conditions which took each of them to the brink of human endurance—fully merits official recognition . . .*

As this book goes to press, Mike is engaged in a coast-to-coast speaking tour (at his own expense) to rally public support for Viet Nam POWs still "Missing in Action." These include the Alliance's Dr. Ardel Vietti and Archie Mitchell and the Mennonite's Dan Gerber.

A Word of Thanks from the Authors

From the outset, Dr. Kenneth Taylor, president of Tyndale House Publishers, took a personal interest in this book. Tyndale House provided for travel to Minnesota, Texas, Georgia, Oregon, Mexico, the Philippines, and Viet Nam for background research and personal interviews with source people. We are also especially grateful for special guidance and assistance from Dr. Victor Oliver, Tyndale's managing editor, and his wife Dixie, who are both former missionaries to Viet Nam.

Mike Benge was, of course, the key source. In tribute to Betty Olsen and Hank Blood and in the desire that their story might become better known, Mike shared painful recollections of their captivity as well as remembrances from his ordeal after their death. Mike's mother also assisted with some interesting incidents from his childhood.

Pastor Ngue, who was interviewed in Pleiku, South Viet Nam, related his experiences with the captives and described his dramatic escape from the Communists. Then a Radê tribal preacher, he is now superintendent of the tribal church district for the National Evangelical Alliance Church of Viet Nam. Several other Radê tribespeople also provided information on the *Tet* massacre at Banmethuot and the early days of Mike's, Hank's, and Betty's captivity.

Hank Blood's wife, Vange, and his mother, Mrs. Helen Blood, of Portland, Oregon, provided us with a complete file of Hank's letters as well as his personal devotional diary. Dave Blood, Hank's translator brother, also gave valuable aid.

Marilyn Olsen, Betty's sister, shared Betty's letters and personal effects. Bill Gothard, president of the Institute in Basic Youth Conflicts, recalled details of Betty's spiritual crisis and how she overcame the problems that were crippling her life before going to Viet Nam. "As Betty applied biblical principles to her problems," Mr. Gothard said, "I saw her emerge as a buoyant, radiant person."

Several Wycliffe and Alliance missionaries gave valuable insights into the personalities and spiritual experiences of Betty and Hank: Dr. Richard Pittman, Julia Supple, Richard Watson, and Milton and Muriel Barker of Wycliffe; and Betty Mitchell, Olive Kingsbury, Dawn Deets, Millie Ade, Ken and Bernice Swain, Lillian Phillips, and Gene Evans of the Alliance mission in Viet Nam. Betty Mitchell remains at Banmethuot, still hoping that her husband Archie, captured in 1962, is alive and will be released. The Swains, Lillian and Richard Phillips, Dr. and Mrs. Robert Green, and two single missionary nurses are also now at Banmethuot, living in homes rebuilt after the 1968 destruction.

Dr. Louis King, director of the Christian and Missionary Alliance's world-wide foreign missions program, and Gerald

Smith, director of public relations for the Alliance, gave enthusiastic support.

Two former POWs, Sergeant Joe Anzaldua and Major Nick Rowe, broadened our understanding of prison life in South Viet Nam. Sergeant Anzaldua also was helpful in telling about his experiences in North Viet Nam where he was incarcerated with Mike Benge.

Sandy Olsen, director of the Corpus Christi, Texas, MIA-POW chapter for the National League of Prisoners' Families, gave good assistance. Mrs. Olsen's brother, Floyd, is still unaccounted for in Viet Nam.

Faye Park typed the final manuscript with her usual commitment of concern for meaning and accuracy.

We thank all of these and others who are not named for their willing assistance. They must share credit with the authors and publisher for whatever inspiration and challenge readers may receive.

To those readers who may wish to make contributions in memory of one or both of the missionaries who died in captivity:

Gifts sent to the Henry Blood Memorial, Wycliffe Bible Translators, P.O. Box 1960, Santa Ana, California 92702, will be used to help pay for the printing of the Scriptures in Vietnamese tribal minority languages.

Funds sent to the Christian and Missionary Alliance, 260 West 44th St., New York, N.Y. 10036, may be designated in Betty Olsen's memory for general missionary work among the Vietnamese people.